FULL MOON SUPPERS

AT SALT WATER FARM

FULL MOON SUPPERS

AT SALT WATER FARM

Recipes from Land and Sea

ANNEMARIE AHEARN

Photographs by Kristin Teig

ROOST BOOKS
Boulder 2017

This book is dedicated to my mother, father,
and sister, who patiently supported me in
my quest to start a business on the same piece
of land that we all call home.

CONTENTS

INTRODUCTION

As a child, I dreaded our summer visits to Maine. The beaches were rocky, the water was too cold for swimming, and every morning the fog lay so thick across the harbor we were sure we would have to spend yet another day at the bowling alley. Our family (going back five generations) owned a blueberry farm in Dresden, but when I was eighteen years old, my parents decided to buy their own land on the Maine coast. My father was fulfilling a lifelong dream; I was, in a word, disappointed.

On a cold and dreary July afternoon, we loaded up our 1981 Volvo station wagon and drove north along the coast on Route 1. At the crest of a hill and across the road from an abandoned motel, my father pulled the wagon over into a shallow ditch. We bushwhacked in muck boots through fallen trees and mud puddles for about ten minutes, and in the distance, through the heavy mist, we caught a glimpse of breaking waves. We could smell the ocean more than we could see it, as flecks of hail spit down on our L. L. Bean raincoats. The seventeen-acre piece of rugged land on which we stood had no buildings, plenty of standing water, and hordes of tumbled-down and decaying trees. Once an old sheep farm, all that was left behind were buried bones and overgrown fields. My father, beaming, put his arms around my sister and me and proclaimed, "Girls, this is where we will spend the rest of our lives." My mother stood beside us, supporting her husband's dream. My sister and I sighed and forced smiles across our faces.

Little did I know that this piece of land in Lincolnville, Maine, would change my life forever, that my greatest love affair was yet to come, and that every thought and every feeling I had from that point on would be fundamentally altered by my new place in the world. Because of this land, I would go on to start a farm with no farming experience, a cooking school in my family's home, and a restaurant in a town with fewer than two thousand people.

After the purchase of the land, my folks built a seaside cottage, where we would spend summers while I was in college. I took jobs in town, working shifts at the local lobster pound as a waitress and later as a prep cook at a little bistro that had acquired national acclaim. I soon noted that the community truly appreciated good local food. When my family decided to sell their home in Wisconsin, we needed somewhere to put all our belongings. My parents built a barn of antique posts and beams, perched on a hillside overlooking Penobscot Bay, and outfitted it with two bedrooms. In 2009, I left New York City and moved to my family's property to live in the new barn. It felt like a wild and undiscovered place. The rough and ragged coastline, exposed by the dramatic tides, seemed inhospitable to new arrivals. My only companions were my fiercely protective Australian shepherds, Moose and Moxie, who were as daunted by our new surroundings as I was. After all, the three of us had been living in a small apartment for years, where familiar sounds were the subway shuddering under-ground and the street sweepers powering down the streets before dawn.

Salt Water Farm

I had not moved to Maine on a whim. My plan was to open a cooking school for home cooks and teach people how to grow a kitchen garden. The mission of the school aligned with my personal ambition, which was to fundamentally change my daily routine. City life, while rich with professional opportunity, did not feed my soul in the way that I was hoping a more rural life would. And what better place to experience nature than on a farm, nestled between the mountains and the sea? So many skills that my grandmothers and generations prior to theirs possessed I did not know the first thing about. Chopping wood for warmth, putting up preserves for winter,

catching a fish for dinner, and raising laying hens for eggs were all efforts that I wanted to experience firsthand.

Browsing at a local bookstore, I came across *One Man's Meat*, a collection of E. B. White's essays. Its pages were filled with observations he had made while living on a farm on the coast of Maine. Like me, he was a city transplant, humbled by the power of nature's elements. One essay, "Salt Water Farm," depicts a walk through a farmer's field to the ocean's edge and notes all the edibles the land and sea provide. Moved by his experience and its resemblance to my own, I named the cooking school Salt Water Farm.

The school opened in the summer of 2009, and my marketing campaign consisted mainly of posting flyers announcing upcoming classes all over the community. The surrounding area has about five thousand year-round residents and an onslaught of visitors between the months of June and October. None of them knew who I was or that I had ambitious plans. My fingers were crossed.

Full Moon Rising

One unusually warm evening in September, beneath a full harvest moon, a new friend and I sat under the stars and proposed initiating a monthly supper club at Salt Water Farm. We planned to offer thoughtful seasonal menus to folks in the community in an effort to celebrate our local food on the night of every full moon. Two months later, we hosted the first Full Moon Supper. It was a cold November evening, and the fire indoors was roaring. We used the pizza oven to cook up Alsatian-style pies (a wonderfully salty combination of Emmental cheese, sweet onions, and smoked bacon). A dear friend brought a real stuffed beaver in celebration of the Beaver Full Moon, named after the Native American tradition of setting beaver traps in late fall; the enormous animal watched over us as we ate. When one of the cooks stepped outside to get more firewood, he noticed a guest's car in the parking lot was ablaze. We called the fire department, and they arrived just in time to put out the twenty-five-foot-tall fire before it licked the roof of the barn. The guests were resilient, committed to our feast, and they all stayed for more wine and four more courses. It was a memorable start to a supper series that continues to be full of surprises to this day.

Since their inception, each Full Moon Supper has paid respect to Native American symbolism, and they are a tribute to the creatures, the elements, and the conditions of the earth as we round the lunar cycle. Our farm table stretches across the dining room and is carefully set for twenty guests. Running down its center are flowers, branches, and vines from the garden and the fields that surround the farm, no matter the season. The menus and tones of each supper reflect not only the bounty of the season but also the spirit of the celebrated moon. For instance, during May's Full Flower Moon, the table is adorned in azaleas and daffodils and the meal begins with a gently fried chive blossom, which the herb garden offers by the dozens. In June, a dessert of cornmeal shortcakes and cream is covered in generous heaps of strawberries, the fruit after which the full moon is named. And in October, a friend stops by just before dinner with a basket of freshly cut mushrooms from the neighboring woods to kick off the Full Hunter's Moon.

A Full Moon Supper is also an acknowledgment of the hard work that goes into food production. Take a moment to give thanks to the sternman hauling lobster traps at 4 A.M. or the farmer working tirelessly to harvest corn before the fall rains. Eating local is not a trend; it's how we nourish ourselves as grateful and thoughtful human beings. Cooking is not work; it is a pleasure and a natural extension of our daily lives. I hope each of you, through reading this book, will be inspired to begin a new tradition of hosting a monthly supper beneath a full and glorious moon, something we can all admire from our place on the earth.

The twelve menus in this book feature my favorite dishes curated from more than one hundred Full Moon Suppers, all celebrated around our farm table with friends, family, and guests from across the globe. Each chapter shares my kitchen notes, seasonal inspirations, and tips on how to gracefully feed large groups. While the suppers at my cooking school feed twenty guests, I've scaled down the menus here to serve a more manageable table of eight.

Full Moon Suppers celebrates feasting with friends; however, the recipes can be used in your everyday cooking repertoire as well. Every savory recipe in this book can stand alone as a meal unto itself, whether as a midafternoon snack, a lunch for two, or a quiet family dinner.

Hosting a monthly supper is a good practice for both seasoned and aspiring home cooks, a means of honing your skills in the kitchen and building your appreciation for seasonal fare. It's also a fine excuse to converse around a beautifully set table and to feast upon food that feeds all the senses.

HOW TO BE
A GRACEFUL HOST

Hosting a dinner party can be daunting. Many of us put an enormous amount of pressure on ourselves to impress our guests, swallowing the stress of a labor-intensive day and forcing a wide smile when the first guest arrives. We must rethink that approach. If you love to cook, as I do, think of the day as an opportunity to spend several hours undisturbed in the kitchen, listening to your favorite music and bringing together a beautiful meal. Your guests are the lucky recipients of a day's work. Hosting Full Moon Suppers has given me ample opportunity to practice feeding many mouths with ease. This chapter guides you through the process of hosting your own Full Moon Supper from start to finish, offering a time-tested strategy for success. My goal is to encourage you to relax, enjoy the day, and feel confident as a host. Like everything, it takes practice, but after a few rounds, you'll find a grace that allows you to sit alongside your guests and savor both their company and the evening's meal.

Cook for the Weather

One's ability to enjoy food is a function of mood, and mood is tied directly to weather. It would be unorthodox (and in poor taste) to make a heavy stew or soup on a hot and humid day, for example. Heat calls for cool flavors and dishes that lift the palate, not weigh it down. Each menu in this book is attuned to the elements outdoors and the resulting sentiment they inspire.

Let the Season Lead

Consider time and place as driving forces in the meal. For each Full Moon Supper I carefully take into account the monthly harvest, whether it be vegetables and herbs from the garden, plentiful fish from the sea, or high-quality meat from the butcher. I often craft my menus with a seasonal cookbook or magazine in hand for inspiration, then weave a succession of dishes together that complement one another.

Texture and Color

Each dish should have a combination of at least two textures and three colors. Contrast in texture allows us to appreciate the physical qualities of each ingredient: crunchy and smooth, crispy and tender, dense and airy, moist and dry. A dish of one shade bores the eye, whereas an orange calendula petal and a few drops of oil can bring a white bean soup to life. In planning our Full Moon Supper menus we consider color throughout, making every effort to brighten each dish while also providing contrasting textures for a pleasing mouth feel.

Portion Control

For multicourse meals, the portions of each dish must be relatively small, or your guests will not be able to get out of their chairs after dessert. No matter how wonderful the meal, discomfort trumps a tasty and memorable dish, so make sure to serve responsible portions.

SERVE LOTS OF VEGETABLES, FEWER GRAINS, AND EVEN LESS MEAT Preparing a meal for more people than we are used to feeding can put us on edge, and we often compensate by purchasing too much food. Here are some general guidelines.

Meat and Fish For a feast that is two, three, or four courses, the proportion of meat in an entrée can be a fraction of what it would be in a one-course meal. The rule of thumb in a multicourse meal is ⅓ pound of protein per person; the only exception is meat or fish on the bone, for which ½ pound is plenty.

Grains A pound of pasta should feed eight people as part of a multicourse menu. Cooked rice and simple grains need not be more than ⅓ cup per person. When serving complex grains such as farro, wheat berries, or barley, serve only ¼ cup per person. Serve no more than a whole medium potato per person.

Vegetables You can never have too many vegetables in preparing for a feast. Many of our Full Moon Supper dishes depend solely on vegetables, and their simple preparation makes for a quick and healthy course that often helps to pace a meal. In the summer and fall, when vegetables are abundant, they find their way into just about every dish at Salt Water Farm.

The Butcher, the Baker, and the Candlestick Maker

Half of being a good cook is knowing how to shop for food. Familiarize yourself with your local farmers' markets and even go a step further: acquaint yourself with the farmers themselves. Farmers are extremely hard workers with minimal profit margins. Knowing that you are grateful for the commitment they have made to growing naturally raised food goes a long way. Ask questions about how things are grown, why the melons are larger this year than last, why the tomatoes are later to the market, why the raspberry season is shorter than usual. Farmers face a variety of challenges every year, and our knowledge of them is as important as our consumption of their food.

It is equally important that you have thoughtful and substantive conversations with your food purveyors. If you don't already, consider starting regular visits to the butcher, whose family has run her shop for generations; the fishmonger, who prides himself on the freshest filets; and the baker, whose time-honored sourdough comes out of the oven not a minute too soon.

Setting the Table

I appreciate simple things and don't outfit my table with imported linens, ornate floral arrangements, or crystal wine glasses. There are a few musts, however. For each meal, I set the table with handmade candles in colors that suit the season. Mismatched napkins are folded hot out of the dryer, making them look pressed (thanks, Mom, for the tip). And no matter the month, I scavenge the fields and woods of the farm for natural growth that brings the outdoors into the dining room. In the summer, I fill mason jars with wild flowers; in the fall, apple blossoms; and in the spring, forsythia. In the coldest months, even winterberries will do. These simple touches are just enough to win the hearts of your guests.

Timing and Organization

THE DAY BEFORE THE SUPPER Do all your ingredients shopping before the day of your feast. This will free you to focus on cooking the day of your gathering, without the aggravation of last-minute errands. There is no greater pleasure for a cook than devoting an entire day to the kitchen, uninterrupted.

THE MORNING OF THE SUPPER Early in the day, generate a to-do list. In the food industry, this is referred to as *mise en place*, which means "putting in place." Include every last detail on the day's list. At the top are the tasks that can be done well ahead of time or take the longest to achieve, such as making dessert. Most desserts can hold up for many hours at room temperature because of their sugar content.

Labor-intensive savory items need to be prepared in the first half of the day: for example, shelling peas, making pasta or pie dough, building a beef stew, mixing a salad dressing, washing greens, preparing sauce or custard. The flavors in these dishes benefit from time spent melding. Try completing these essential steps by noon.

MIDDAY To shift my focus, I usually set the table around noon. When an entire day is devoted to the same objective, it's important to keep a schedule that is both fluid and fluctuating. This keeps the mind interested, making each task enjoyable rather than laborious. Count your guests once, twice, and three times. Make sure the seats are dusted, the silverware is polished, and the glassware is sparkling. Set the center of the table with a bit of woven seasonal brush, flowers, vines, or branches. Place a handmade candle between every four guests.

BETWEEN NOON AND DINNERTIME You can save yourself loads of last-minute preparation by precooking certain foods hours ahead of time: poaching eggs, grilling meats and vegetables, and precooking shellfish. Many proteins can be cooked and allowed to rest (out of the refrigerator) for about four hours before serving. (The refrigerator will rapidly dry out whatever it holds, so try to avoid storing precooked proteins in it.) When it's time to serve them, the proteins need just a blast of heat to create a little color on top and to achieve the correct doneness.

Complete every task before taking a break. Harvest some edible flowers from the garden for garnish, bring together a batter for frying, taste and adjust the seasoning of a stew, or crumble cheese for a salad. Leave for later only the things that must be done immediately before the meal, such as slicing fresh tomatoes, mincing herbs, dressing lettuce, and frying.

TWO TO THREE HOURS BEFORE GUESTS ARRIVE Perhaps the most import step: take a break. Go for a walk. Stretch your legs. Give yourself enough time to get ready. A proper host must look as well prepared as her or his meal. Without a mental and physical break from the kitchen, the quality of the day deteriorates.

ONE HOUR BEFORE THE SUPPER Hors d'oeuvres should be served at room temperature, so there is no need to fuss over them when your guests arrive. All cheeses and meats need to come out of the refrigerator a full hour before they are served to make sure they are flavorful.

AS GUESTS ARRIVE When the guests arrive, they almost always ask if there is anything for them to do. They want to contribute in some way, despite the fact that it's not their kitchen. And so I always leave a couple of tasks for them. Something clean and easy, like picking parsley or putting ice in glasses. Assigning tasks also acts as an icebreaker. It prevents guests from just sitting around and gets them moving about the room, which is a more comfortable dynamic for most people.

THROUGHOUT THE EVENING Clean as you go, whether it's during the preparation or the presentation of the meal itself. If possible, ask for help during the feast, either from a partner or a paid assistant, so that you can sit and enjoy the meal that you've created. If you are on your own, allow a little time between courses to do a quick clean (I guarantee some of your guests will give you a hand) before moving onto the next course.

You now have the tools necessary to get started. Pick a date for your Full Moon Supper, invite your friends, and commit to the itinerary. Most important, relax. Forgive yourself for mistakes you make along the way—they are inevitable—and remember never to take this whole entertaining thing too seriously. If you're not having fun, what's the point?

A NOTE ON DRINKING

Every meal should begin with a well-made drink, or a "sundowner," as the British call it. Knowing how to make a winning cocktail is as important as cooking the meal itself, as cocktails create the guests' very first impression. Mixology requires only two things: a good recipe and the proper implements.

First, chill your glassware (and make sure that you're using the correct glassware for the drink). Second, use the right implements: a jigger to accurately measure the ingredients, a long spoon for stirring, and a cocktail shaker with a built-in strainer. Keep plenty of ice on hand and fill the shaker all the way to the top with cubes. A lovely garnish goes a long way in exciting the eye and can be prepared ahead of time.

Test out new cocktail recipes beforehand so there are no surprises at supper. When entertaining large groups, consider preparing a pitcher's worth for your guests and allow 1½ drinks per person. Add plenty of ice at the last minute and stir. Now you are free to greet your guests, pour them a drink, and concentrate on the execution of the meal. (I suggest you help yourself to a libation as well.)

~Full Moon Supper at Salt Water Farm~

July 12th, 2014

A Taste of

English Peas and Their Shoots, Tide Mill Ricotta
& Pine Nuts on Country Toast

First Course

Garbanzo Bean Soup, Aliums, Amish Filed Tomatoes, Fennel,
Baby Squash, Saffron

Second

Speckled and Frilled Lettuces, Chopped Farm Eggs, Local
Bacon, Lemon Thyme Vinaigrette

Third

Commonwealth Farm Chickens, Grilled Broccoli and Red
Onions, Grange Corner Farm Stone Ground Grits

To Finish

Strawberry Galettes, Whipped Elderflower Cream

Tips for our Services are Very Much Appreciated

THE
MENUS

JANUARY

●

THE FULL

WOLF MOON

In the month of January, deep snow covers the ground, the wild winds building drifts so high that fences become obscured. Under layers of ice, lake fish swim freely and catch the fishermen's lines. At night, the scent of food, alive or dead, can carry for miles, drawing scavengers across town borders.

It is a desolate time in the wild, but a peaceful time for more domesticated creatures. January is a month for rest and relaxation in the purest of forms. Those of us who make a living on the coast of Maine work tirelessly from May to October so that, come January, we can put our feet up by the fire with a glass of cider or bourbon and flip through a 600-page novel at leisure, guilt-free. Such seasonal cycles take some getting used to, but once your body and mind adapt, it's a wonderful life. Like the waning and waxing moon, we gather energy and strength in the winter for the summer's frenzied exertion. But un-

like the scavenging wild animals of the night, all winter long, we humans feast!

January's Full Wolf Moon honors the hungry wolves that howl for sustenance outside villages, their bellies empty. From inside our heated homes, their sound reminds us to be grateful for our stocked pantries and refrigerator doors and, of course, shelter.

In the depths of winter, we can also be grateful for the generosity of the sea. Beneath cold waters are schools of delicious fish that many cooks argue are at their finest in January. Sea urchin are harvested in enormous quantities during their short winter season, lobsters are full of richly flavored meat, and cod is plentiful. Citrus, which so naturally complements seafood, is featured throughout the January Full Moon Supper. To balance the lightness of fish and the acid of oranges and lemons, a decadent cream-based gnocchi graces the table, and a comforting rice pudding finishes the feast.

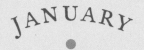

JANUARY
·

FULL MOON SUPPER
MENU

Vodka Martini
*with a Vermouth Rinse and
a Twist of Lemon*
29

Sea Urchin Butter on Toasts
30

Potato Gnocchi
*with Lobster, Cream, and
Tarragon*
33

Roasted Beets
*with Citrus, Horseradish Yogurt,
and Toasted Hazelnuts*
36

Poached Codfish
*with Green Olives, Fennel,
Saffron, and Tomato Conserva*
39

Cinnamon Rice Pudding
*with Cara Cara Oranges, Medjool
Dates, and Wildflower Honey*
43

Vodka Martini
with a Vermouth Rinse and a Twist of Lemon

Every host should know how to make martinis, whether or not you drink them. Once you understand the basic recipe, you can add a little olive juice, splash in a touch more vermouth, or drop in a cocktail onion.

MAKES 1 DRINK

dry vermouth for rinsing

2 ounces vodka

1 strip of lemon peel

Rinse a chilled coupe or martini glass with vermouth and pour the excess into the sink. Fill a bar glass to the top with ice and add vodka. Stir with a bar spoon and strain the vodka into your coupe or martini glass. Drop a strip of lemon peel in the center.

Sea Urchin Butter on Toasts

Sea urchin must be eaten fresh. As a result, it may be a difficult ingredient to come by. It is prized in Japan, and most of the catch from the United States is shipped across the Pacific. A good sushi restaurant will have a source for sea urchin and may recommend it to you if you ask.

Many call sea urchin "the butter of the sea," and one of my favorite presentations of urchin is in compound butter on sourdough toast. The butter will have a rich, earthy flavor and shouldn't taste overwhelmingly of fish.

Opening an urchin is as challenging as opening an oyster. The desired tool for such an operation is a pair of kitchen shears or a sea urchin opener (rather hard to find in this country).

MAKES UP TO 20 TOASTS

12 unshelled sea urchins (or 4 ounces if out of their shells)
16 tablespoons (2 sticks) unsalted butter, softened
sea salt
1 loaf sourdough bread

With kitchen shears, cut open the sea urchin around what would be the equator on a globe, wearing gloves to protect your hands. Expose the inside of the urchin. Remove the orange morsels and rinse in water.

Gently fold the cold sea urchin into the butter until evenly incorporated. Sprinkle generously with sea salt. Place in the fridge until 20 minutes before you're ready to serve. Allow the compound butter to soften a bit at room temperature.

Cut the loaf of sourdough bread in half and then into thick slices. Toast under a broiler or place on a grill for a minute or two on each side, until grill marks appear. Spread each piece generously with sea urchin butter. Serve warm.

> **SEA URCHIN** can be bought out of its shell at Japanese seafood markets. If you cannot procure sea urchin, many canned fishes will make an excellent compound butter. These include sardines, kippers, and anchovies. Each will yield a different flavor but are equally delicious.

Potato Gnocchi
with Lobster, Cream, and Tarragon

In winter, lobsters migrate far out to sea. They are typically hard-shelled during deep winter, because it is not safe for them to molt at such great depths and in close proximity to so many deep-sea predators. If you are a hard-shell lobster lover, this is a wonderful time of year to incorporate meaty lobster parts into a meal—especially when smothered in homemade lobster stock, cream, and pillowy pasta.

For this recipe, you'll use the claws, knuckles, and tail meat. Save the legs for a snack. The bodies are used to make the stock, along with the remaining shells and any clear juice that you collect over a bowl when you open up the lobsters. Tomalley (the lobster's greenish liver) and eggs will discolor the sauce and stock, so try to keep them separate.

)

SERVES 8 TO 10

4 lively 1¼- to 1½-pound
   lobsters

2 pounds russet potatoes,
   peeled and quartered

2¾ cups all-purpose flour

3 eggs, lightly beaten

kosher salt

2 yellow onions, peeled and
   roughly chopped

4 carrots, roughly chopped

4 celery ribs, roughly
   chopped

1 tablespoon olive oil

2 cups white wine

1 fresh bay leaf

2 sprigs thyme

2 sprigs parsley

2 sprigs rosemary

12 black peppercorns

4 tablespoons butter

4 shallots, peeled and
   minced

continued on next page

Fill a large pot with 2 inches of heavily salted water. (It should mimic seawater; taste it.) Once it's come to a boil, put your lobsters in the pot and cover. Steam the lobsters for 6 to 8 minutes and check for doneness: once they've turned red, they need only another minute or so. (They are being partially cooked, as they will continue to cook in the lobster sauce.) Remove the lobsters from the pot, let them cool enough for you to handle them, and remove meat from shells. Cut the meat into bite-size pieces.

Place the potatoes in a large pot with heavily salted water to cover and bring to a boil. Reduce to a simmer and cook the potatoes for 25 minutes, or until tender. Drain and let cool. Pass the potatoes through a ricer onto a clean flat surface. Mound in a pile, then create a well in the center. Add flour and eggs to the well. Salt generously with the kosher salt. Using a fork, gradually incorporate the eggs and flour into the riced potatoes until a dough begins to form. Knead by hand until the dough feels soft and pillowy and has a consistent texture.

Divide the dough into 6 portions. Roll each portion into a ½-inch rope, about a foot in length. With a bench knife, cut pasta dough every ½ inch. Using the back of a fork or a gnocchi imprinter, roll pieces along

1 shot Cognac or brandy

2 cups cream

6 sprigs fresh tarragon,
    leaves picked from stems
    and stems discarded

the tines or wood to imprint them with ridges. Flour a
cookie sheet and collect the gnocchi on the sheet.

In a stockpot, toss the onions, carrots, and celery in
the olive oil and a good pinch of salt, cover, and sweat
over medium-low heat for 10 minutes. Add the empty
lobster shells and bodies, white wine, bay leaf, herbs
(except for the tarragon sprigs), and peppercorns.
Barely cover with water, bring to a boil, then reduce
to a simmer. If foam rises to the top, skim off with a
slotted spoon and discard. Let the stock cook for 30
minutes. Your kitchen should smell heavenly. Strain
into a small saucepan and begin to reduce stock over
medium heat.

In a large frying pan, sweat the minced shallots in
2 tablespoons of the butter until soft and translucent.
Deglaze with the Cognac or brandy (if you're using a
gas stove, turn the flame off to prevent a fire). Turn the
heat back to high and cook off the alcohol, 2 to 3
minutes. Add the cream and 4 cups of lobster stock to
the pan and let simmer for 5 minutes. Stir in the lobster
meat and remaining 2 tablespoons of butter.

Bring a new large pot of generously salted water to
a boil. Working in batches, add gnocchi and cook until
just tender, about 5 minutes. Using a slotted spoon,
transfer gnocchi to the lobster sauce and toss gently.

Plate the gnocchi in small bowls, ladling lobster
meat and more sauce over the top. Garnish with
tarragon.

Roasted Beets
with Citrus, Horseradish Yogurt, and Toasted Hazelnuts

While citrus does not grow in Maine, oranges, lemons, and grapefruit are at their peak in more southern regions in January. A variety of segmented citrus in combination with roasted beets and horseradish cream makes for a rather decadent and colorful winter salad, perfect for offsetting January's monotone landscape.

SERVES 8

6 red beets, greens and
   tails trimmed
2 cups water
5 tablespoons olive oil
1 tablespoon white wine
   vinegar
⅓ cup hazelnuts
1 garlic clove, peeled
kosher salt
1 tablespoon Dijon mustard
1 lemon, supremed,
   remaining juice squeezed
   from the rind and pith and
   set aside
1 orange, supremed,
   remaining juice squeezed
   from the rind and pith and
   set aside
½ cup Greek yogurt
1 tablespoon grated fresh
   horseradish
red pepper flakes
fresh ground pepper
1 large grapefruit, peeled
   and cut in ¼-inch-thick
   rounds
seeds of ½ pomegranate
1 large bunch Italian flat-leaf
   parsley, leaves picked from
   stems and stems discarded

Preheat the oven to 375°F. In a baking dish, combine the beets, water, 1 tablespoon olive oil, and the white wine vinegar. Cover with foil. Bake or steam in the oven for 45 minutes, or until beets are fork-tender. Drain, peel under cold water, and set aside.

Turn the oven down to 350°F. Lay the hazelnuts on a baking sheet. Toast them in the oven for 8 minutes, or until they become fragrant. Remove from the oven, let cool, and then chop each nut in half.

To make a dressing, use a mortar and pestle to mash the garlic clove with a big pinch of salt until it becomes a paste. Add Dijon mustard and citrus juice; whisk in the remaining olive oil.

In a small bowl combine yogurt and horseradish. Add salt, pepper, and red pepper flakes to taste.

Spread yogurt mixture on a large platter. Lay grapefruit segments over the yogurt. Arrange beets on top, then supremed orange and lemon segments. Drizzle a few spoonfuls of dressing over the top. Toss parsley leaves with a couple spoonfuls of dressing and sprinkle on top of the beets and citrus. Spoon the remaining dressing around the outside of the beets. Garnish with pomegranate seeds and toasted hazelnuts. Serve at room temperature.

HOW TO OPEN A POMEGRANATE

The easiest (and neatest) way to open a pomegranate is under water. Begin by whacking the pomegranate with a wooden spoon, or rolling it firmly on a hard surface to release the seeds— you will hear them make a slight popping sound. Cut an "X" at the top of the pomegranate and squeeze the juice out into a small bowl. Next, cut or pry the pomegranate in half and put it in a large bowl of cold water. Holding the pomegranate under the water, break the fruit into rough segments and begin releasing the seeds from the pith a few at a time. The seeds will sink to the bottom of the bowl, and the pith will float to the top. Scoop out the pith with your hands and then drain the seeds.

Poached Codfish

with Green Olives, Fennel, Saffron, and Tomato Conserva

With a few pints of canned tomatoes from last summer's harvest and a pinch of saffron, a good cook can bring the warmth of the Mediterranean to the table even on the coldest of days.

SERVES 8

FOR THE TOMATO CONSERVA

4 vine-ripened tomatoes

4 garlic cloves, gently smashed and left in their skins

3 tablespoons olive oil

kosher salt

FOR THE POTATOES

16 fingerling potatoes

2 tablespoons olive oil

4 garlic cloves, gently smashed and left in their skins

1 bunch Italian flat-leaf parsley, stems removed and leaves roughly chopped

FOR THE POACHING LIQUID

2 yellow onions, peeled and thickly sliced

1 tablespoon butter

1 tablespoon olive oil

kosher salt

4 garlic cloves, peeled and roughly chopped

2 fennel bulbs, stalks and hearts removed and bulbs thickly sliced

continued on next page

TO MAKE THE TOMATO CONSERVA Preheat the oven to 375°F. Cut fresh tomatoes into 8 wedges each. Line a sheet pan with parchment paper and arrange the tomatoes in a single layer across the bottom. Add the smashed garlic cloves and coat everything in the olive oil. Shake the pan to make sure the tomatoes are well coated. Sprinkle generously with salt. Bake until the tomatoes begin to caramelize on the bottom, about 12 minutes. Flip each tomato and return the pan to the oven for 8 minutes. Tomatoes should be sweet, sticky, and partially dehydrated.

TO MAKE THE POTATOES Fill a 2-quart saucepan with the potatoes and heavily salted water. Bring to a boil and cook over high heat until tender, about 15 to 20 minutes. Drain. In a large frying pan, heat the olive oil, add the garlic cloves in their skins and the potatoes, and sauté over medium heat until the potato skins start to brown, about 15 minutes. Add half the parsley leaves and toss together, reserving the other half for garnish. Turn off the heat and let the mixture rest on the stovetop.

TO MAKE THE POACHING LIQUID In a large, ovenproof stew pot, sweat the onions in the butter, olive oil, and a good pinch of salt over medium-low heat. Add the roughly chopped garlic and continue to sweat over medium-low heat for 10 minutes. Add the fennel and cook for 10 minutes longer, or until the vegetables are translucent and broken down. Stir in the canned tomatoes, saffron, bay leaves, and red pepper flakes. Continue to cook over medium-low heat until the tomatoes break down and some of the liquid reduces,

1 quart canned, whole,
    peeled San Marzano
    tomatoes
10 saffron threads
2 bay leaves
1 pinch red pepper flakes
1 cup Sauvignon Blanc

FOR THE FISH
2 pounds cod or halibut
1 lemon, thinly sliced
kosher salt
fresh ground pepper
½ cup Castelvetrano olives

about 25 minutes. Add the wine and simmer for at least 15 more minutes, until the alcohol evaporates.

TO MAKE THE FISH Preheat the oven to 375°F. Divide the fish into eight equal portions. Place each piece of fish in the tomato sauce; top each with a thin lemon slice. Sprinkle with kosher salt and a few grinds of pepper. Bake for 12 to 15 minutes, or until fish is just cooked through. (The hot liquid will continue to poach the fish after it comes out of the oven.)

To serve, spread the potatoes onto a large platter. Transfer the fish to the platter with a spatula and spoon the poaching liquid over the top. Garnish with tomato conserva, Castelvetrano olives, and the remaining chopped parsley.

Cinnamon Rice Pudding

with Cara Cara Oranges, Medjool Dates, and Wildflower Honey

No dessert is more comforting than a bowl of cinnamon-scented rice pudding, with a touch of booze to relax the belly. A few brightly colored orange slices and a pile of dates add a little sophistication to the presentation.

SERVES 8

1 cup flame raisins

1 cup Calvados

1 cup water

¾ cup jasmine rice, uncooked

½ teaspoon kosher salt

2 cups half-and-half

½ cup light brown sugar

2 cinnamon sticks

1 egg

1 teaspoon vanilla extract

4 Cara Cara oranges, peeled and sliced into rounds

sea salt

wildflower honey

16 Medjool dates

Soak raisins in Calvados for 30 minutes. While they are soaking, prepare the rice: In a medium saucepan, combine water, jasmine rice, and kosher salt. Bring to a boil, cover, and cook for 6 to 8 minutes. Add half-and-half, brown sugar, and cinnamon sticks. Cook over medium heat, stirring every couple of minutes, until the rice is fully cooked, 15 to 20 minutes. In a small bowl, beat the eggs lightly. Add a few spoonfuls of hot rice to the eggs and stir to incorporate. Then stir the egg and rice mixture into the rice pudding and continue cooking for 1 to 2 minutes. Remove from heat. Stir in vanilla extract until fully incorporated. Let cool, cover, and place in the fridge.

Drain the raisins. Portion the rice pudding into individual bowls, garnish each with a sprinkling of raisins, and serve. Lay orange slices out on a large platter. Sprinkle with a little sea salt, drizzle with honey, and nestle the dates beside. Place the family-style orange platter at the center of the table. Make sure that everyone has a small plate for the fruit.

FEBRUARY

•

THE FULL

HUNGER MOON

The February full moon is named for the heavy snow and weather that make hunting for food extremely challenging. It is called the Full Hunger Moon, as by this time of year many animals have dwindling supplies of nourishment. In the early morning, after yet another snow, I can often see animal tracks across the fields, circling round the compost pile, and trailing underneath the chicken coop in my yard. The northeastern Abenaki tribe called the February moon *Piaodagos*, or the "Makes Branches Fall in Pieces Moon." I can attest to this phenomenon, having once watched an old apple tree split in half and fall on top of my vegetable garden, crushing a hand-built fence.

For those of us who reside mostly indoors during this time of year, creativity in the kitchen becomes paramount. Cold days give us plenty of time to lay decorative tapestries and linens across the table, flip through cookbooks from around the world, experiment with foreign or unfamiliar culinary techniques, and take on consuming projects such as making marmalade, braising tough cuts of meats, and soaking and simmering beans.

In February we also celebrate the delights of ice fishing, pickles and preserves from the pantry, root vegetables from our cellars, local meats packed tightly in the freezer, and the exotic spice cabinet that sees little action during more fruitful months. Deep winter gives us the perfect excuse to cook with vibrant spices and condiments like turmeric, saffron, and harissa, which add color and dimension to a winter meal.

As in many cold coastal regions, Maine has a strong culinary tradition of preserving fish. Generations ago, excess haddock led people to smoke haddock fillets, called "finnan haddie," which would last months on a long sea journey. Another strong tradition in colder climes is preserving meat for use all year. When an animal is harvested in the fall and freezer packed, by February you may be left with some of the less desirable (a relative term) or slower-cooking cuts. Flavorful stews are a testament to the richness that can be coaxed from even the toughest cuts of meat.

February's Full Moon Supper menu is both a tribute to the winter culinary traditions of New England and a celebration of time spent gathering recipes and inspiration from foreign lands to create dishes that bring welcome warmth, color, and flavor to a cold climate.

•

FULL MOON SUPPER
MENU

Up to Snuff
47

Finnan Haddie Fritters
with Rouille
48

Scarlet Runner Beans
with Harissa, Tomatoes, Kale,
Preserved Lemon, and Mint
51

Jerusalem Artichokes
with Parsley, Bacon,
Watercress, and Grain Mustard
55

Braised Lamb Ribs
with Apricots, Moroccan
Spices, and Saffron Rice
56

Marmalade Cake
with Crème Fraîche
59

Up to Snuff

As this menu begins with a Catalan-inspired dish, it seems appropriate to pair it with a sherry-based cocktail, a beverage I became all too familiar with while spending time in Andalusia, Spain. Sherry warms both body and soul and should always be of the dry variety.

MAKES 1 DRINK

1½ ounces manzanilla
  sherry
1 ounce Bulleit rye
½ ounce Cointreau
1 drop sherry vinegar
1 strip of lemon peel

Fill a bar glass to the top with ice and add all the ingredients except the lemon peel. Stir with a bar spoon and strain into a chilled coupe glass. Drop a strip of lemon peel in the center.

Finnan Haddie Fritters
with Rouille

This recipe, inspired by Colman Andrews, the editor in chief of *Saveur* magazine when I interned there, pays homage to the tradition of preserving fish, along with an ingredient essential to Maine's economy: the potato. It's served with a rich rouille, which in French means "rust colored," imparted by the smoked paprika (*pimentón*).

SERVES 8

FOR THE ROUILLE

1 large garlic clove

2 pinches kosher salt

2 egg yolks

1 cup olive oil

1 teaspoon lemon juice

1 pinch smoked paprika

FOR THE FRITTERS

1½ pounds finnan haddie

1 bay leaf

kosher salt

3 medium Yukon Gold
   potatoes, peeled and
   diced

1 cup water

2 tablespoons olive oil

¾ cup flour

3 eggs

2 garlic cloves, peeled and
   minced

4 sprigs parsley, finely
   chopped

fresh ground pepper

10 cups vegetable oil

TO MAKE THE ROUILLE With a mortar and pestle, mash the garlic with a pinch of salt until it becomes a paste. Add the egg yolks and beat with the pestle until the yolks lighten in color. (You can cheat by adding a spoonful of store-bought mayonnaise, so your rouille doesn't break.) Slowly add the olive oil, drop by drop, vigorously stirring the mixture with the pestle until it is emulsified into a mayonnaise. Once the mayonnaise has thickened, continue stirring vigorously and add the remaining oil in a thin, steady stream. Add the lemon juice, the second pinch of salt, and smoked paprika. Taste and adjust seasoning if necessary.

TO MAKE THE FRITTERS In a frying pan, cover the finnan haddie and bay leaf with cold water, then bring to a simmer. Simmer for 20 minutes, or until the fish becomes tender enough to flake. Remove the fish and let cool. Flake the fish into very small pieces, discarding any bones and skin.

Fill a large pot with water and salt it generously. Add the potatoes and turn the heat to high, bringing it to a boil. Cook the potatoes until tender, 15 to 20 minutes, then drain and discard the water.

In another pan, bring 1 cup of water and the olive oil to a boil. Remove from heat and slowly whisk in the flour to form a batter. Beat in the eggs, one at a time. The batter will be loose and slippery until the eggs are fully incorporated. Make sure it thickens before the addition of each egg.

In a large bowl, mix together the finnan haddie, potatoes, minced garlic, and parsley. Season to taste with salt and fresh ground pepper. Blend the batter into the fish mixture. Season to taste again. The batter should be thick enough to shape into loose balls with two spoons. If it's too thin, add some additional flour.

Before you begin frying, have a slotted spoon or a spider ready and a sheet pan lined with paper towels for the fritters to drain on. Place a little bowl of kosher salt near your sheet pan.

Pour at least 3 inches of vegetable oil into a medium saucepan. Bring the oil to 350°F over medium heat. Test the temperature with a little batter (or the tip of a parsley sprig) to see if the oil sizzles. Form finnan haddie batter into little footballs with 2 spoons. Push them off the spoon into the oil and fry them in batches of four, never crowding the pan. (Every time you drop cold batter into the oil, the oil temperature drops, so you may need to adjust the heat during frying to keep the oil at 350°F.) When the fritters are golden brown on top, flip them over and let them brown on the other side. Then, remove them to the sheet pan and sprinkle a little salt on top while they are still hot.

Serve the fritters hot with rouille on the side, for dipping.

Scarlet Runner Beans

with Harissa, Tomatoes, Kale, Preserved Lemon, and Mint

Serious home cooks plan the major culinary events of the day either while still lying in bed or as they put the kettle on for their morning cup of coffee. If you intend to serve properly soaked and stewed beans for dinner guests, you must start the process the night before. For this recipe, if you can't find scarlet runner beans, you can order Rancho Gordo scarlet runner beans online.

)

SERVES 8

2 cups dried scarlet runner beans, soaked overnight

1 yellow onion, unpeeled and quartered

4 garlic cloves, smashed and left in their skins

3 sprigs thyme

1 bay leaf

1 tablespoon kosher salt, plus more for seasoning

2 tablespoons butter

2 tablespoons olive oil

2 sweet onions, peeled and thinly sliced

4 garlic cloves, peeled and thinly sliced

2 tablespoons harissa

2 quarts plum tomatoes, squished by hand until they are broken up

1 bunch Tuscan kale, ribs removed and leaves cut into thin strips

fresh ground pepper

6 sprigs Italian flat-leaf parsley, leaves picked from stems and roughly chopped

continued on the next page

In a large stockpot, cover the soaked beans with plenty of water. Add the yellow onion, garlic, thyme, bay leaf, and salt. Cook over medium heat for up to 1½ hours, or until tender but not soft. Drain the beans and remove the onion and garlic, reserving the cooking liquid, and let cool.

In a heavy saucepan, melt the butter with the olive oil over medium heat. Add the sliced sweet onions and a pinch of salt and cook, covered, until soft and translucent, about 20 minutes. Add the sliced garlic and cook for an additional 5 minutes. Add harissa and mash into the onions with the back of a wooden spoon. Cook for 3 to 4 minutes, stirring constantly. Add tomatoes and 2 cups of the bean cooking liquid and bring to a simmer. Let cook down for 30 to 40 minutes, until the sauce has thickened slightly. Add the beans, then stir in the kale. Season to taste with salt and pepper.

Serve beans in shallow bowls and garnish with parsley, mint, and a sprinkling of minced preserved lemon.

6 sprigs mint, leaves picked
from stems and cut into
thin strips
1 tablespoon minced
preserved lemon

NOTES ON MAKING
PERFECT BEANS

Beans are rustic and elegant; they have a great purpose in the kitchen. If treated properly, they will add integrity to a dish, even become its star.

- Soak dried beans overnight in a big ceramic or glass bowl, allowing them to absorb water and slowly swell to their original size.
- Always rinse beans fully of the soaking water, then cook them in plenty of fresh, well-salted water.
- Throw in aromatics: a couple of smashed, unpeeled cloves of garlic, a bay leaf, maybe an onion fragment, skin and all.
- As is true for any good winter cooking, cook the beans slowly and at a low temperature. Never rush beans; allow them a full hour and a half to wake in simmering water.
- Monitor the beans' texture carefully. For most dishes, a bean should still have some resistance against the tooth and must not be cooked to mush.

Jerusalem Artichokes
with Parsley, Bacon, Watercress, and Grain Mustard

While Jerusalem artichokes are not quite ready to be harvested in Maine in February, they have been liberated from the earth in warmer locales and often appear in supermarkets this early in the season. They are a prolific perennial, putting out more and more spuds each year, their plant matter growing as high as eight to ten feet in the summertime. They can be eaten thinly shaven, raw, or cooked—like a potato—and, as in this case, sautéed in bacon fat. For some folks, Jerusalem artichokes are hard to digest, so serve them sparingly.

SERVES 8

16 Jerusalem artichokes

8 strips thick-cut bacon,
    cut into ½-inch pieces

2 bunches watercress

1 bunch Italian flat-leaf
    parsley

1 garlic clove, peeled

kosher salt

2 tablespoons grain mustard

zest and juice of 1 large,
    juicy lemon

1 tablespoon sherry vinegar

¼ cup olive oil

fresh ground pepper

Fill a large saucepan with salted water and bring to a boil. Scrub the Jerusalem artichokes with a stiff brush and remove any particularly thick skins or nubs. Once the water is boiling, add them to the pot. Cook until fork-tender, about 15 minutes. Don't overcook them; they will fall apart. Slice each Jerusalem artichoke into ½-inch-thick pieces.

In a large cast-iron skillet, fry the bacon over medium heat until the fat is rendered and the bacon begins to get crisp. With a slotted spoon, transfer the bacon onto a paper towel. Place the Jerusalem artichoke slices in the pan with the bacon fat and cook over medium heat until they brown on one side. Flip them over and brown the other sides. They should be crispy on the outside and tender in the middle. Once they are cooked, turn off the heat and leave them in the pan.

Trim the lower half of the stems from each bunch of watercress. Wash and dry thoroughly in a salad spinner. Pick all the parsley leaves from the stems. Wash and dry thoroughly in the salad spinner.

With a mortar and pestle, grind the garlic clove with a pinch of salt. Add the mustard, lemon zest, lemon juice, sherry vinegar, and olive oil. Season with salt and pepper to taste.

Plate Jerusalem artichokes on a large platter and drizzle with some dressing. Top with watercress and parsley. Sprinkle with bacon pieces and 2 spoonfuls of dressing, reserving extra dressing for another use. Just before you are ready to serve, gently toss the greens.

Braised Lamb Ribs

with Apricots, Moroccan Spices, and Saffron Rice

Lamb, strong in flavor and its ribs coated in a thick layer of fat, stands up wonderfully to the mélange of Moroccan spices. In this dish, the apricots absorb the savory stew while maintaining their tartness.

SERVES 8

FOR THE LAMB

2 tablespoons olive oil

5 pounds lamb ribs

kosher salt

fresh ground pepper

3 yellow onions, peeled and
   thinly sliced

5 garlic cloves, peeled and
   thinly sliced

2 tablespoons tomato paste

¾ teaspoon cinnamon

¾ teaspoon cumin

½ teaspoon coriander

8 cups lamb or beef stock

1 bay leaf

2 cups dried apricots

FOR THE RICE

2 tablespoons butter

1 shallot, minced

kosher salt

pinch of saffron threads

1 tablespoon peeled and
   minced fresh turmeric or
   1½ teaspoons dried
   turmeric

2 cups uncooked jasmine rice

4 cups water

zest of 1 lemon

1 small bunch mint, leaves
   picked from stems and
   stems discarded

TO MAKE THE LAMB In a large sauté pan, heat the olive oil over medium-high heat. Season the lamb ribs generously on both sides with salt and pepper. Brown the ribs on both sides, making sure to get them crispy, about 5 minutes on the first side and 3 minutes on the second. Remove them from the pan to rest.

Turn the heat down to medium low and add the onions and a pinch of salt and cover. Cook until the onions are translucent and beginning to caramelize. Add the garlic and cook for an additional 5 minutes. Mash the tomato paste into the onions with the back of a spoon and cook for 3 to 4 minutes, stirring constantly. Add cinnamon, cumin, and coriander and stir to incorporate. Return the lamb ribs to the pan and pour in enough stock to just cover the ribs. If there is not enough stock to cover them, top off with water. Add bay leaf and apricots. Bring to a boil, then reduce heat to a simmer, partially cover, and cook for 2½ hours, or until rib meat is tender and falling off the bone. (You can also finish the lamb in a 325°F oven.)

TO MAKE THE RICE In a medium saucepan, melt the butter over medium-low heat. Add the shallot and a pinch of salt and sweat until the shallot is tender, 8 to 10 minutes. Add saffron and turmeric and cook for 5 more minutes, or until turmeric has softened. Add rice and toss to coat with the butter and spices. Toast rice for 1 minute, moving it around in the pan with a wooden spoon. Add water and bring to a boil. Reduce to a simmer, then cover and cook for 20 to 25 minutes, or until all the water has been absorbed and the rice is fully cooked.

Serve lamb ribs and sauce over saffron rice on a platter. Garnish with lemon zest and mint.

Marmalade Cake
with Crème Fraîche

This wonderfully rich, orange-scented cake is the perfect final note to a vibrant and exotic meal. Served with a sour crème fraîche, it will make your mouth pucker with delight. If you're short on time, you can replace the homemade marmalade with a high-quality store-bought one.

SERVES 8

FOR THE MARMALADE

5 seedless oranges

1 lemon

4 quarts water

4 cups sugar

FOR THE CAKE

1½ cups cake flour

½ cup cornmeal

2 teaspoons baking powder

1 teaspoon kosher salt

¼ teaspoon ground
   cardamom

8 tablespoons (1 stick)
   butter, softened

¾ cup sugar

3 eggs

2 cups marmalade

1 teaspoon vanilla extract

1 cup heavy cream

¼ cup crème fraîche

confectioners' sugar
   (optional)

TO MAKE THE MARMALADE Cover the oranges and lemon with the water in a big pot. Turn the heat on high, cover, and boil for 2 hours. Turn off the heat and let the citrus and water cool overnight. Your entire home will smell of sweet and wonderful oranges.

The next day, remove the oranges and lemon from the cooking liquid, reserving liquid. Cut each orange in half, scoop out the flesh, and put it into a glass bowl. Slice the lemon in half, and do the same, holding back the seeds. With your hands, break up the orange segments. Slice the orange peels into thin strips and put them in the bowl with the flesh. Stir, then return the mixture into the pot with the cooking liquid. Add the sugar, stir, and place the pot over high heat. Cook until the mixture has reduced by two-thirds or until the marmalade has set, about 45 minutes. Marmalade can be made up to two weeks ahead of time.

TO MAKE THE CAKE Preheat the oven to 350°F. Butter and flour a 9-inch springform pan. Line the base with a circle of parchment paper.

In a medium bowl, combine the flour, cornmeal, baking powder, salt, and cardamom. Set aside. In a stand mixer with a paddle attachment, whip the butter and the sugar on medium speed until light and fluffy. Add the eggs one at a time, beating to fully incorporate each egg. Beat in 1 cup of the marmalade and the vanilla extract on low speed. With the mixer continuing on low speed, add a third of the heavy cream to the batter, then add a third of the dry ingredients; keep adding in thirds, alternating ingredients, until batter is well blended. Stop the mixer occasionally to scrape down the sides of the bowl.

Pour the batter into the prepared pan. Bang it a few times on the counter to release any air bubbles. Set the pan on a sheet tray to catch any overflowing batter. Bake for 1 hour. Check for doneness by inserting a toothpick. If the toothpick comes out dry, the cake is done. If not, bake for up to another 10 minutes. When done, remove from the oven and let cool for 5 minutes on a wire rack. Release the cake from the springform pan by unlatching the side of the pan, inverting the pan onto a plate, then reinverting the cake onto a cake plate. Let cool completely.

Serve each slice with a generous spoonful of marmalade on top of the cake and another spoonful of crème fraîche on the side. Dust each slice with confectioners' sugar, if you'd like.

BAKING THE PERFECT CAKE

It requires some careful observation to bake a perfect cake, as every recipe and every oven are different. Always check the cake 20 minutes into the bake time to ensure that it's cooking evenly. If it's gaining color too quickly on top but the batter is still loose in the middle, move an oven rack above the cake and slide a sheet tray on top of it. This will allow the cake to continue to bake without browning any further. As a general rule of thumb, when the cake has set, allow it to cook for another 2 to 3 minutes and then remove it from the oven to cool.

MARCH

●

THE FULL

CROW MOON

March's Full Crow Moon is the last full moon of winter, when the crows begin to caw and the earth begins to thaw. Worms wiggle up through the frigid soil, and robins return to their nests. In New England it is also called the Full Sap Moon, as this is the time of year when maple trees release their golden sap, which has been harvested and boiled down into syrup in sugar shacks for generations. On Maple Sunday in late March, an unofficial regional holiday, all the sugar shacks have their doors open, the fires roaring, and giant pots of sap bubbling and slowly reducing into liquid gold.

The March moon is known as the Full Crust Moon, in reference to the top layer of snow that melts in the day and freezes at night. Although the nights are still cold and another snowstorm (or two or three) is certain, longer daylight assures us that spring is around the corner. Not spring in the traditional sense—flowers blooming and warm rains—but spring in that the snow will melt, the earth will soften, and the lakes will thaw.

Maine does not see its first green growth until well into April, and even then the offerings are small and precious. As the earth yields little bounty in March, I draw culinary inspiration from a great Irish celebration: St. Patrick's Day. The climate and terrain of Maine and that of Ireland are quite the same: fog as thick as pea soup; rocky, ragged coastlines; fields of green; cool temperatures for most of the year, with a short stretch of blessedly warm months. Irish food is as good as its excellent raw ingredients; Maine's is much the same. Like Ireland, Maine is home to an astonishing variety of fish and shellfish. Both Ireland and Maine have ample land for the grazing of livestock and green pastures from the favorable amount of rain, allowing for the production of high-quality meat and milk. Because of their long winters, both the Irish and Mainers have a strong tradition of growing storage crops, such as root vegetables, cabbage, and winter squash. And finally, of critical note, both demographics cultivate a particular skill set to carry them through winter: brewing and distilling.

There is a heartiness to the March Full Moon Supper menu, which is comprised of a collection of dishes rich in history and culture. You often hear chefs from Maine who have worked all over the world say, "For some reason, the food just tastes better here." It is no miracle but rather terroir that is responsible for this. Smoked fish, brown bread, and maple syrup are all Maine winter staples. March is a time to embrace the last of winter cooking in the comfort of our warm kitchens.

MARCH

●

FULL MOON SUPPER
MENU

A Pint of Stout
65

Smoked Mackerel
with Pickled Cucumbers
and Brown Bread
66

Celery Root Slaw
with Fennel and Apple
69

Fresh and Smoked
Haddock Chowder
70

Braised Beef and Stilton Pie
73

Bread and Butter Pudding
with Bittersweet Chocolate
and Maple Syrup
76

A Pint of Stout

There is something almost nourishing in each sip of thick stout. It's not as heavy as one might think and certainly not as alcoholic as some of the craft beers so common today. I'd go so far as to say that if I were to drink a beer for breakfast, it would most certainly be a pint.

SERVES 1

One 14.9 ounce can Guinness (or other favorite stout)

Chill a pint glass. Slowly pour the stout beer into the glass until it's two-thirds full. Wait 2 minutes. Fill to the top. Serve.

Smoked Mackerel
with Pickled Cucumbers and Brown Bread

This fanciful little appetizer is a celebration of not one, not two, but three New England traditions: brown bread cooked in a can, smoked fish, and pickled vegetables. While mackerel makes for a flavorful spread, trout or salmon could be used instead. You'll need two empty, clean 12-ounce cans to bake the bread in traditional form, or you can use an 8-by-8-inch baking dish to make a loaf.

☽

SERVES 8

FOR THE BROWN BREAD

2 tablespoons unsalted
   butter

2 tablespoons flour

½ cup corn flour

½ cup rye flour

⅔ cup white flour

½ teaspoon baking powder

¼ teaspoon baking soda

1 pinch toasted fennel seed

½ teaspoon kosher salt

1 egg

½ cup molasses

½ cup milk

FOR THE CUCUMBERS

½ large English cucumber,
   peeled

½ cup apple cider vinegar

2 tablespoons olive oil

1 pinch kosher salt

1 pinch red pepper flakes

1 squeeze fresh lemon

FOR THE SMOKED MACKEREL

8 ounces smoked mackerel

⅓ cup crème fraîche

2 spring onions, finely
   chopped

continued on p. 68

TO MAKE THE BROWN BREAD Preheat the oven to 300°F. Butter and flour two clean 12-ounce cans. In a bowl, combine the flours, baking powder, baking soda, fennel seed, and salt and whisk together. In a separate bowl, beat the egg with molasses and milk. Create a well in the center of the dry ingredients and pour in the wet. With a whisk, slowly incorporate the flours into the wet ingredients until the resulting dough is even in texture.

Pour the dough into the cans and cover tightly with aluminum foil. Place the cans in a warm-water bath in a deep ovenproof dish, making sure that the water is about an inch below the tops of the cans. Bake for 2 hours, or until the bread is cooked through. To check, insert a toothpick into the center of the bread, and if it comes out clean, the bread is ready. Place the cans on a rack to let cool completely.

TO PREPARE THE CUCUMBERS Finely slice the cucumber into rounds. (You can use a mandoline for this.) In a small bowl, mix together the apple cider vinegar, olive oil, salt, red pepper flakes, and squeeze of lemon. Place the cucumber rounds in the brine and let pickle for 20 minutes.

TO MAKE THE SMOKED MACKEREL In a medium glass bowl, break up the mackerel into tiny pieces with your hands. Add the crème fraîche, spring onions, chives, lemon juice, pinch of salt, and a few twists of the pepper mill. Mix thoroughly. Taste and add salt if needed.

1 very small bunch chives,
 finely chopped
1 tablespoon lemon juice
1 pinch kosher salt
1 pinch fresh ground pepper

To create a family-style platter, slide the brown bread out of the cans and cut into ½-inch rounds. Lay them across a cutting board and place a dollop of fish spread on top of each along with a few pickled cucumbers. Serve at room temperature.

Celery Root Slaw
with Fennel and Apple

Who says root vegetables can't be eaten raw? A clever tool called a mandoline (or exceptional knife skills) can slice a root so thinly that it is not only digestible in its raw form but delicious, adding crunch to a salad or slaw. This slaw can be made a few hours ahead of time, but if it spends too much time sitting in the bowl it will begin to weep.

SERVES 8

2 garlic cloves, peeled

kosher salt

1 tablespoon Dijon mustard

¼ cup crème fraîche

2 tablespoons sherry
  vinegar

fresh ground pepper

1 pinch red pepper flakes

¼ cup olive oil

juice and zest of 1 lemon

2 celeriacs, tough outer
  layer cut away

2 Granny Smith apples,
  cores removed

2 fennel bulbs

1 head Bibb lettuce

With a mortar and pestle, grind the garlic cloves with a big pinch of kosher salt until they become a paste. Mix in the mustard, crème fraîche, sherry vinegar, ground pepper, red pepper flakes, and olive oil to make a dressing.

Place the lemon juice and zest in a separate medium bowl. Using a very sharp knife or a mandoline, slice the celeriac and apple into matchstick-size pieces and add them to the lemon juice, giving them a good toss to prevent browning. Then pick a dozen small fronds from the fennel and reserve for garnish. Cut the fennel bulb away from the stalks and discard the stalks. Cut out the heart of each bulb and discard. Thinly slice the remaining bulb into matchsticks. Add the dressing to the vegetables, stir, and let sit for 20 minutes so the slaw absorbs the flavors. Taste and season with more salt and pepper if needed.

When ready to serve, place one or two large leaves of Bibb lettuce on each salad plate. Spoon a tight little nest of the slaw on top. Garnish with trimmed fennel fronds.

Fresh and Smoked Haddock Chowder

Traditional New England chowder is typically a thick, almost gelatinous soup that sticks to your gut and fills your belly. I have always preferred the Irish version, which is made with milk. This recipe is a happy medium, calling for 1 cup of cream and a sprinkling of flour, which adds a bit of body without creating a soup that sticks to your spoon.

SERVES 8

1½ pounds finnan haddie (if unavailable, use salt cod)

6 strips unsmoked bacon (use smoked bacon if using salt cod)

2 yellow onions, peeled and diced

4 leeks, greens removed, cut in half lengthwise and then across into thin half moons

6 celery ribs, cut thinly

½ teaspoon kosher salt

2 tablespoons all-purpose flour

8 cups fish stock

2 cups reserved finnan haddie cooking water (or salt cod water)

2 large waxy potatoes, diced, skin on

2 bay leaves

1 cup cream

1½ pounds fresh haddock, cut into bite-size pieces

2 tablespoons cold butter

red pepper flakes or fresh ground pepper

½ bunch Italian flat-leaf parsley, leaves picked from stems and roughly chopped, stems discarded

In a large pan, cover the finnan haddie with water and bring to a simmer on the stovetop. Cook for 20 minutes, or until the fish has softened. Remove each fillet with a slotted spoon and let cool on a plate. Reserve 2 cups of cooking liquid. When the fish has cooled, flake the fillets into small pieces and set aside. Discard bristly bits.

Cut the bacon into ½-inch pieces and fry in a large soup pot over medium heat. Move the bacon around once the fat begins to render to prevent sticking. Stir every couple of minutes, until bacon begins to get crisp and the fat is fully rendered. Add onions, leeks, celery, and salt. Cover and cook until the onions are translucent and vegetables have softened. Add the flour and give the mixture a good stir to coat all the vegetables. Cook for a few minutes, toasting the flour. Add the fish stock, finnan haddie cooking water, potatoes, and bay leaves and turn the heat to high until the chowder begins to boil. Lower the heat to medium and cook for 10 minutes, until the potatoes begin to soften. Add the finnan haddie and the cream and continue to heat at medium for about 5 minutes, never letting it reach a boil. Add fresh haddock and cook for another 5 minutes. Add nubs of cold butter to finish. Season with red pepper flakes or black pepper for added spice.

Serve in individual bowls and add a generous sprinkling of chopped parsley over the top.

Braised Beef and Stilton Pie

This recipe has only a top crust and is thus best suited for servings in individual crocks; you will need eight to ten ovenproof crocks. As part of a multicourse meal, a meat pie with a double crust might be too filling. But if the meat pie is being served alone, by all means, double the crust recipe and surround the filling with buttery pastry!

SERVES 8 TO 10

FOR THE BEEF STEW

2 tablespoons olive oil

3 pounds stew beef (shoulder or rump), cut into 1-inch cubes

kosher salt

fresh ground pepper

flour for dredging

2 large onions, diced

8 carrots, cut into 1-inch diagonal pieces

8 celery ribs, cut into 1 inch diagonal pieces

4 garlic cloves, peeled and minced

2 tablespoons tomato paste

few shakes Worcestershire sauce

1 tablespoon Dijon mustard

1 bouquet garni (made by tying together 1 large sprig thyme, 1 sprig rosemary, 2 parsley stems, and 1 bay leaf)

1 pound yellow potatoes, peeled and chopped into ½-inch cubes

8 cups beef stock

one 14.9-ounce can Guinness stout

continued on next page

TO MAKE THE BEEF STEW In a large stewing pot, heat the olive oil over medium heat. Season the beef cubes with salt and pepper, dredge them in flour, and brown them in batches, using a set of tongs to transfer each piece to a plate when done. Don't overcrowd the pot, or the beef will steam rather than brown. Sweat the onions, carrots, and celery in the stew pot until soft. Add the garlic and continue cooking until the vegetables start to gain color. Mush the tomato paste into the vegetables. Cook for 2 to 3 minutes, or until the mixture continues to gain color. Add the Worcestershire sauce and the Dijon mustard and stir to fully incorporate. Return the meat to the pot and add the bouquet garni, potatoes, beef stock, and Guinness and bring to a boil. Reduce to a simmer, cover, and cook for at least 2½ hours and up to 3 hours, until the beef is tender. Taste and season. Discard the bouquet garni. Add the peas and cook for 2 minutes, just long enough to heat them through. To finish the stew, swirl the butter into the sauce and sprinkle with parsley leaves. Let cool completely. The stew should be thick, with enough liquid so it won't dry out in the oven. If it seems too thick, add ½ cup of water.

TO MAKE THE CRUST Combine the flour and salt in a mixing bowl. With a pastry cutter, cut in the cold butter until the mixture resembles coarse cornmeal. Sprinkle with just enough ice water so the dough holds together when worked with your hands, about 3 tablespoons. Shape into two equal-size balls, wrap them in plastic, and refrigerate for 20 minutes.

1 cup frozen green peas

2 tablespoons unsalted
    butter

½ bunch Italian flat-leaf
    parsley, leaves picked
    from stems and stems
    discarded

FOR THE BUTTER CRUST

2½ cups all-purpose flour

1 teaspoon kosher salt

16 tablespoons (2 sticks)
    cold unsalted butter

ice water

½ pound Stilton cheese,
    broken up into about
    16 pieces

4 tablespoons butter, melted

TO MAKE THE PIES Preheat the oven to 375°F. Between two sheets of parchment paper, roll out each ball into a 12-inch round about ⅛ inch thick. Lay as many crocks as you can fit, rim side down, on top of the dough. Trace around the rim of each crock with a sharp paring knife. Pull away the excess dough and roll it out again to a ⅛-inch thickness. You should be able to get a pie top for each crock. Fill each crock with braised beef and a few chunks of Stilton. Lay a round of crust over the top of each crock and press the dough against the edges. Punch a hole in the center of the crust for steam to escape. Brush with melted butter.

Arrange the crocks on 2 sheet pans and bake for 45 minutes. Rotate the pans after about 20 to 25 minutes so heat distributes equally and to ensure even browning. Let cool for 10 minutes before serving.

RECIPE VARIATION: DOUBLE-CRUSTED PIE

To make one 9-inch double-crusted pie: Preheat the oven to 375°F. After rolling out the dough into two 12-inch rounds, ⅛ inch thick, lay one crust in a pie dish and chill it for about 10 minutes. Fill the crust with beef stew, place the hunks of Stilton on top, and cover with the second crust. Press the edges of the two crusts together and crimp in a decorative pattern with the tines of a fork or your fingers. Brush with melted butter. Place the pie dish on a sheet pan and bake for 1 full hour.

Bread and Butter Pudding
with Bittersweet Chocolate and Maple Syrup

A little bakery that doubled as a dinner restaurant in New York City used to lure me in with its chocolate bread and butter pudding. It was finished in a wood-fired oven (word has it, the oldest in the city), and the edges were extra crispy, the bread soaked in butter, cream, and presumably rum. This dish is my interpretation.

SERVES 8

8 medium-thick slices good-quality sourdough bread

1 cup bittersweet chocolate chips

8 tablespoons (1 stick) butter

4 eggs

4 cups cream

¾ cup plus 2 tablespoons maple syrup

1 teaspoon vanilla extract

¼ teaspoon grated nutmeg

½ teaspoon grated Mexican cinnamon stick or ground cinnamon

pinch kosher salt

confectioners' sugar for dusting

Cut the bread slices into quarters, then put half of them back together like puzzle pieces to fit as snugly as possible in a 7-by-7-inch casserole dish. Sprinkle the chocolate chips over the first layer. Configure a second layer of bread on top.

Preheat the oven to 375°F. In a medium saucepan, melt the butter. Brush the top layer of bread generously with about 6 tablespoons of butter and reserve the remainder. Break the eggs into a glass bowl and give them a good whisk. Add 2 cups of the cream and ¾ cup of maple syrup, the remaining butter, vanilla extract, nutmeg, cinnamon, and salt. Whisk together thoroughly, then pour the mixture over the bread, pressing the slices down so they soak up the egg mixture. Place the casserole dish into a slightly larger baking dish or roasting pan and fill the larger pan with water to about 1 inch below the top of the smaller dish. Bake until the custard is set and the top of the bread is golden and puffed up, about 50 minutes. Cut into squares.

In a clean bowl, whip together the remaining 2 cups of cream and 2 tablespoons of maple syrup. Serve the pudding warm with a spoonful of whipped cream and a dusting of confectioners' sugar.

APRIL

•

THE FULL

EGG MOON

April's full moon is named for the egg production of birds, symbolizing new growth, fresh starts, and the earth revealing itself once the snow has melted. It is also called the Full Fish Moon, as the rivers swell with alewives and trout headed out to sea. Cormorants hover above the waters, waiting for a meal, spreading their wings in magnificent display. The lakes thaw, and the creeks and streams fill with melted snow, which makes its way down the rolling hills and into the ocean.

On cool April mornings, wearing a pair of tall rubber boots, I'll walk along the coastline with the dogs, looking for edibles. Speckling the big, smooth rocks that make up our beach are little periwinkles, cobalt blue when wet and often spotted with a baby barnacle or two. Small mussels grip the rocks with their wiry beards, their flesh enough for a nibble rather than a full bite.

Where the bluff meets the shore are a number of edible wild greens flavored by the salty mist. In the spring, sea spinach sprouts up on the hillside and makes a wonderful addition to a salad of greens. Along the stream edges are groves of watercress, tender and peppery. Dandelion greens begin to pop up everywhere, a young, tender addition to a soup, salad, or grain dish. Lovage, sorrel, and chives grow an inch a day in herb gardens. Coltsfoot begins to crawl around the outside of the barn, and baby arugula and spinach brave the cool nights, ingredients for the finest salads of the year. Nettle abounds and can be cooked down into a creamy soup or sizzled atop a pizza in a wood-fired oven.

Our April Full Moon Supper menu is flush with new growth, both wild and from the garden. The resurgence of eggs from the chickens yields a salad of soft-cooked yolks on a bed of tender greens. Sweetened root vegetables find purpose in a pureed soup garnished with sea spinach. A simple lemon tart with a slathering of fresh whipped cream finishes the meal—and, just like that, we've turned our backs on winter.

APRIL

●

MENU

Two-Inch Punch
81

Periwinkles
Cooked in Seawater
82

Overwintered Parsnip Soup
with Garlicky Sea Spinach
84

Soft Egg, Baby Radishes, Tender
Wild Greens, and Ricotta Salata
87

Braised Rabbit
with Fennel, Leeks, Dijon, and
French Lentils
88

Lemon Curd Tart
with Fresh Whipped Cream
92

Two-Inch Punch

This cocktail's peculiar name comes from a game that children play to test their strength. The rule is as follows: you are allowed no more than two inches' draw to punch your friend in the arm as hard as you can. I'm not sure if there is a direct correlation between the action of the game and the drink, but perhaps it refers to the feeling you have the next morning after you've had one too many.

)

SERVES 1

1 ounce Hornitos Silver
   tequila
¾ ounce Aperol
½ ounce New Orleans
   bitters
1 bar spoon maraschino
1 bar spoon oleo-saccharum
cava topper (or other
   sparkling wine)
1 strip of orange peel

Fill a bar glass to the top with ice and add the tequila, Aperol, bitters, maraschino, and oleo-saccharum. Stir with a bar spoon and pour into a wine glass with the ice. Top with a small pour of cava or some other bubbly, and garnish with orange peel.

Periwinkles Cooked in Seawater

Collecting periwinkles, or "winkling" by the shore, is best accomplished with many hands (from many friends). For those who don't live on the coast, this dish can be made with store-bought mussels, using the same preparation. Make sure they are extremely fresh; your nose will tell you if they aren't.

SERVES 8

2 cups periwinkles in their
    shells
4 tablespoons butter
1 shallot, peeled and minced
2 garlic cloves, peeled and
    minced
pinch kosher salt
1 shot dry sherry
1 cup seawater or heavily
    salted water
4 sprigs parsley, leaves
    removed from stems
    and finely chopped,
    stems discarded
crusty bread

Place periwinkles (or mussels) in a bucket of cold fresh water for 1 hour, then drain. If you are using mussels, give them a good cold rinse with cold water, but do not submerge them.

In a large saucepan or frying pan, melt the butter over medium heat. Add the minced shallot, garlic, and salt. Cook until softened. Turn off the flame, add the sherry, then turn the flame back up to medium. Let the alcohol cook off, about a minute or two. Add seawater or salted water and bring to a boil. Add the periwinkles and let simmer for 6 to 8 minutes. Place the pan on a trivet. Garnish periwinkles with parsley. Serve with crusty bread for dipping and toothpicks to remove the meat from the shells.

Overwintered Parsnip Soup
with Garlicky Sea Spinach

While this soup can be cooked with grocery store parsnips and a bag of spinach from the greens aisle, it is made particularly sweet by overwintered parsnips and tender young wild spinach.

If you're a gardener curious about overwintering crops, leave a row of turnips in the ground through the winter and harvest them when the ground thaws in the spring. What better gift is there, after a long winter, than a fresh vegetable?

SERVES 8

2 tablespoons butter

3 tablespoons olive oil

2 large yellow onions, peeled and diced

kosher salt

3 garlic cloves, peeled and minced

16 overwintered parsnips, peeled and chopped into ½-inch rounds

8 cups vegetable stock

2 sprigs thyme

1 bay leaf

kosher salt

fresh ground pepper

red pepper flakes (optional)

4 cups well washed, gently packed spinach (sea spinach or locally grown)

sea salt to finish

In a large soup pot, melt the butter and 2 tablespoons of the olive oil over medium heat. Add diced onions and a pinch of kosher salt. Cover and sauté for 15 to 20 minutes, or until onions are translucent. Add 1 minced garlic clove and sauté uncovered for an additional 5 to 10 minutes, until the garlic is tender and smells milder. Add the parsnips, stock, thyme, and bay leaf. Bring to a boil and then reduce to a simmer. Cook until parsnips are tender, 20 to 25 minutes. Turn off heat and remove the thyme and bay leaf.

Let cool for at least 15 minutes and then, in a blender or food processor, puree the soup in batches until smooth, making sure not to fill the blender to the top. Generously salt and pepper each batch and add stock from the pot to get the right consistency. (I often blend each batch with a pinch of red pepper flakes, adding a kick.) Transfer each batch to a medium saucepan, or any vessel that will fit 12 cups of soup.

In a large frying pan, heat the remaining olive oil and minced garlic. Add the spinach and a good pinch of kosher salt and cook just until the leaves wilt. Remove from the heat.

To serve, slowly warm the parsnip soup over medium-low heat. Ladle into individual bowls. Place a little nest of garlicky spinach at the center of each bowl. Sprinkle with sea salt. Serve with crusty bread.

Soft Egg, Baby Radishes, Tender Wild Greens, and Ricotta Salata

The beauty of this salad is that is can be made with a variety of greens and even, in some instances, weeds. You don't need to be an expert forager to visit a field in the springtime and pick a few dandelion leaves. Radishes are so young and tender this time of year that even their greens are edible. A baby radish (or radish thinning from the garden) can be carefully washed, then cut in half lengthwise, greens and all, and added to the salad.

$\smile$

SERVES 8

4 farm-fresh eggs

16 to 20 small radishes (preferably French Breakfast or Cherry Belle)

6 loosely packed cups spring greens (arugula, young dandelions, coltsfoot, watercress, spinach, purslane, mizuna)

I garlic clove, peeled

kosher salt

zest and juice of 1 lemon

2 tablespoons sherry vinegar

1 handful spring herbs (sorrel, lovage, chives), finely chopped

⅓ cup olive oil

fresh ground pepper

⅓ pound ricotta salata, shaved into about 20 long strips with a vegetable peeler

Fill a medium saucepan halfway with cold water. Place the eggs in it, bring to a boil, and boil for 2 minutes. Remove the eggs from the pan and run under cold water in the sink. Peel the eggs carefully and set them aside.

Clean the radishes and cut them in half, keeping the greens attached if they are small and tender. Rinse and dry the spring greens and place them in a salad bowl. With a mortar and pestle, grind the garlic clove with a pinch of salt until it resembles a paste. With the pestle, coat the inside of the mortar with the garlic paste. This step helps the garlic flavor penetrate the dressing. Add the lemon zest and juice and the sherry vinegar and stir with the pestle. Add herbs and olive oil and stir again, then season with salt and pepper to taste and set aside for 20 minutes so the flavors can meld.

Gently toss the greens with about 2 tablespoons of the salad dressing. Carefully slice the eggs in half. Place a nest of greens on each plate. Add 3 to 4 halved radishes around the base of the nest and lay half of an egg, yolk facing up, on the side. Place a few shavings of ricotta salata across the greens and add a spoonful of dressing around the outside of the plate, to allow your guests to draw more salad dressing into the greens as desired.

Braised Rabbit

with Fennel, Leeks, Dijon, and French Lentils

While rabbit is not as commonly eaten in the United States as it is in many other countries, there is no denying that it is a more ethically raised meat than chicken, lamb, or beef. Moreover, because of their short gestation period, a pair of rabbits can produce more than 600 pounds of healthy, lean meat a year, whereas a single steer carcass yields only about 400, making raising these animals much easier on the environment than raising cattle. I would also argue that it is a tastier white meat than chicken, more complex and richer in flavor. I challenge you to cook it at home, if you haven't before. If you don't see it at your butcher shop, ask if they can special-order it for you. Have the butcher either split the rabbits lengthwise or cut them up. Reserve the carcasses for stock.

SERVES 8

FOR THE RABBIT (OR CHICKEN) STOCK

1 tablespoon olive oil

1 yellow onion, peeled and roughly chopped

tops of 4 leeks, roughly chopped

2 carrots, roughly chopped

2 celery ribs, roughly chopped

kosher salt

2 rabbit carcasses (upper spine and neck) or 1 chicken carcass

2 sprigs thyme

2 sprigs rosemary

2 sprigs parsley

1 bay leaf

12 black peppercorns

FOR THE BRAISED RABBIT AND LENTILS

3 tablespoons olive oil

2 tablespoons butter
continued on p. 91

TO MAKE THE STOCK In a large, heavy stockpot, warm the olive oil and add the onion, leek tops, carrots, celery, and a touch of salt. Cover and sweat the vegetables over medium-low heat until they soften, 10 to 12 minutes. Place the rabbit carcasses (or chicken carcass) in the pot and just barely cover with water. Add herbs, bay leaf, and peppercorns. Bring to a boil, then reduce to a simmer. With a slotted spoon, remove any foam that rises to the top. Simmer for 45 minutes to 1 hour. Strain and let cool. Store in the fridge and use the stock within 3 days or freeze for up to 6 months.

TO MAKE THE BRAISED RABBIT AND LENTILS Preheat oven to 400°F. In a large Dutch oven, warm 1 tablespoon of the olive oil and 1 tablespoon of the butter over medium-high heat. Pat the rabbit meat dry with a paper towel. Season each piece with kosher salt and fresh ground pepper, then dredge in flour, tapping off any excess. Working in batches, brown each piece on both sides in the Dutch oven over medium-high heat, using tongs to flip them over, and set them aside on a plate to rest. Add leeks and two of the chopped shallots to the pan, along with a pinch of salt and a splash of the wine. Stir to loosen all the bits on the bottom of the pan. Turn the heat down to medium and cook until the

MAKING HOMEMADE STOCK

A good homemade stock is the base of every soup, sauce, and stew, and stock from a box simply will not cut it. If you are in the habit of buying whole animals, throwing away the carcass without making a stock is shameful. Historically, making stock was an economic necessity, a means of stretching a portion of meat as far as possible. After a chicken is roasted, the body can be tossed into a pot with some aromatics, a carrot or two, a stalk of celery, a sprinkling of peppercorns, a bay leaf, and a handful of fresh herbs. Making stock is not highly technical. It is no different than making a tea; you are steeping flavorful ingredients in hot water and then straining the solids out. When you're preparing food, save carrot tops, onion skins, leek greens, and celery leaves in the fridge to use for your own vegetable stock.

2 rabbits, cut into eight pieces

kosher salt

fresh ground pepper

all-purpose flour for dredging

4 leeks, white and light
   green parts cut in half and
   then in thin half moons

4 shallots, peeled and finely
   chopped

1 cup Sauvignon Blanc

1 heaping tablespoon Dijon
   mustard

6 cups homemade rabbit
   or chicken stock (see p. 88)

1 bay leaf

4 sprigs thyme

2 fennel bulbs, stalks and
   hearts removed and bulbs
   cut into large chunks

1 lemon, cut into thin rounds

3 garlic cloves, smashed and
   left in their skins

2 cups French lentils, rinsed

6 cups water (or additional
   stock)

4 sprigs each tarragon,
   parsley, and chervil,
   leaves removed from
   stems and stems
   discarded, for garnish

aromatics soften, about 10 minutes. Add the mustard and massage it with a spoon into the vegetables until they are evenly coated. Reintroduce the rabbit pieces to the pan, plus the remaining wine, enough stock to barely cover, the bay leaf, and 2 sprigs of thyme. Place in the oven for 45 minutes to 1 hour. Season to taste with salt and pepper.

Line a sheet pan with parchment paper. Spread the fennel chunks and lemon slices across the pan, then add the smashed garlic cloves and remaining 2 sprigs of thyme. Generously sprinkle with salt and then douse with the remaining 2 tablespoons of olive oil. With your hands massage the salt and oil into the fennel and lemon. Roast for 20 to 25 minutes, or until the fennel begins to caramelize and darken at the edges. Remove from the oven and set aside.

In a medium saucepan, melt the remaining tablespoon of butter over medium-low heat. Add the remaining shallots and a pinch of salt and cook until soft, 7 to 10 minutes. Add dry lentils and 6 cups of water or stock and bring to a boil. Reduce to a simmer and cook for 25 to 30 minutes, or until the lentils are just tender and have absorbed the water fully. Salt to taste.

To serve, spoon the lentils onto a large serving platter. Distribute fennel and lemon across the lentils. With a pair of tongs, place rabbit pieces on top of the fennel. Spoon sauce over top. Garnish with tarragon, parsley, and chervil leaves.

Lemon Curd Tart
with Fresh Whipped Cream

Everyone loves a well-made lemon tart. The lemon curd must be neither too tart nor too sweet, and the crust must be buttery and melt in your mouth. For the topping, I prefer freshly whipped cream to meringue, which can be too sweet and is difficult to make beautiful without a culinary blowtorch.

SERVES 8

FOR THE CRUST

1¾ cups flour

2 tablespoons sugar

½ teaspoon salt

12 tablespoons unsalted
   butter, chilled and cut
   into pieces

ice water

FOR THE LEMON CURD

6 eggs

1 cup sugar

juice of 3 lemons

12 tablespoons cold butter

FOR THE TOPPING

1 pint heavy cream

1 tablespoon sugar

TO MAKE THE CRUST In a large bowl, combine flour, sugar, and salt. Cut the butter into the dry mixture until it resembles coarse meal. Sprinkle with just enough ice water to make the dough hold together, about 3 tablespoons. Form dough into a ball, wrap in plastic, and refrigerate for 20 minutes.

Preheat the oven to 350°F. Transfer dough to a lightly floured surface, then roll it into a 10-inch round. Ease dough into a 9-inch tart pan, pressing it into place with your fingers. Prick the bottom with a fork, cover with aluminum foil, and chill for at least 20 minutes. Fill the foil-lined tart shell with pie weights or dried beans and bake for 15 minutes. Remove weights and aluminum foil and bake for 10 more minutes, or until crust is dry and has set. Set aside to cool.

TO MAKE THE LEMON CURD In a medium saucepan, combine the eggs and sugar and whisk by hand until fully incorporated. Place over medium heat. Add the lemon juice and continue to whisk. When the mixture begins to thicken, in 6 to 8 minutes, add the butter, one tablespoon at a time, until it melts. Whisk continuously for an additional 6 to 8 minutes, or until the curd thickens substantially. Remove from the heat and let cool. Refrigerate for 1 hour. Pour the curd into the tart shell and place in the fridge for another hour to set.

TO MAKE THE TOPPING In the bowl of a stand mixer, combine the cream and sugar. Beat until stiff peaks form.

Once the lemon tart has set, top with whipped cream. Slice and serve.

PERFECT
TART DOUGH

The keys to making perfect tart and pie crusts are to keep the dough cold (which means using cold unsalted butter and ice-cold water), to add just enough water to bring the dough together, and to work quickly. A pie dough that is too hydrated will not flake; rather, it will tear. Pie dough can be made with a variety of fats (lard, butter, shortening), but I prefer a traditional French butter crust, made with fresh butter and a heavy hand of salt. For this lemon tart, a touch of sugar makes the dough more malleable. A pie dough must be cold when it enters the oven, as a warm dough has a tendency to shrink. Always place dough in the refrigerator to chill for 10 to 20 minutes before baking.

MAY

●

THE FULL

FLOWER MOON

The May moon honors fertility in all of its forms; as such, it is also called the Mother's Moon. Warmer temperatures at night make it safe for the young to come into the world, for the earth to protect new growth, and for flowers to bloom. The farm takes precedence in the month of May, as the ground has thawed and it is time to transplant seedlings from the greenhouse into the soft, workable soil.

There is a small harvest in May. The herb garden begins to thrive, and young and tender chives, sorrel, and lovage are ready for collection. The heartier and more savory herbs, such as sage, rosemary, and thyme, green up and conceal winter decay. The asparagus beds are flush with spears. Rhubarb turns a deep shade of red, its leaves broadening and spreading. Greens of all kinds love the month of May for its perfect growing conditions: cool and wet with a few bursts of sunshine but never too much heat. They are much larger and more established than in April but still tender. They fill a salad bowl in no time.

May feels like the perfect month for eating outdoors. The days are relatively long, but the summer heat has not yet set in. There is still time to gather with friends and family before everyone's busy summer schedule takes over. It's a fine excuse to get together to toast the long-awaited warmer weather and blissfully long hours of daylight.

The May Full Moon Supper menu is a taste of a traditional Salt Water Farm asado, an Argentine tradition—akin to a Sunday barbecue—in which a whole animal is cooked over an open fire. The meal begins lightly, with fried chive blossoms in honor of the flower moon, and then heads straight to the fire. There is nothing more flavorful than grilled fresh asparagus in the month of May, and doctoring them too much would be a sin. As a midcourse, young, earthy beets and their greens are paired with a tangy chèvre and fried garlic, followed by the main affair, grilled spring lamb, doused in a lemony herb oil. And, finally, we celebrate the tart perennial that loves colder climates—rhubarb—in a galette made with crushed hazelnuts. This is a meal best served family-style, right up until the dessert, which can be plated.

MAY

•

FULL MOON SUPPER
MENU

Lovage Gin and Tonic
99

Chive Blossom Fritters
with Lemon Mayonnaise
100

Grilled Asparagus
with Farm Eggs and Grated
Hard, Salty Cheese
103

Baby Beets and Beet Greens
with Fried Garlic and Chèvre
104

Grilled Spring Lamb and
Salsa Verde
with Smashed Potatoes and
Alfonso Olive Tapenade
107

Rhubarb Galette
with Hazelnut Crust and
Vanilla Ice Cream
110

Lovage Gin and Tonic

Lovage grows to mammoth heights in May, begging for any and all culinary applications. It tastes similar to celery but is far more intense and can be used only sparingly, which makes it difficult to use up the harvest of even a single plant. After one sip of this cocktail, your guests will be intrigued by the flavor—not just of the lovage but also of the Hendrick's gin, which is infused with rose and cucumber.

)

SERVES 1

FOR THE LOVAGE SYRUP

2 cups sugar

2 cups water

8 cups roughly chopped
   lovage

FOR THE COCKTAIL

2 ounces Hendrick's gin

¾ ounce lovage syrup
   (see recipe above)

tonic topper

lime wheel

TO MAKE THE LOVAGE SYRUP Combine the sugar with water in a saucepan and bring to a boil over high heat. Drop the chopped lovage leaves into the syrup, remove from the heat, and allow to cool completely while the lovage steeps. Strain, pour into a quart jar, and cover. The syrup can be kept in the fridge for up to 3 months.

TO MAKE THE COCKTAIL Fill a bar glass to the top with ice and add Hendrick's gin and lovage syrup. Stir with a bar spoon and pour into a chilled highball glass with the ice. Top off with good tonic and garnish with a wheel of lime.

Chive Blossom Fritters
with Lemon Mayonnaise

I was delighted the first time I realized a chive blossom was edible. It's the perfect combination of a floral and a mild onion taste, and when fried, it holds its magnificent texture and crunchiness. Think of these fritters as sophisticated onion rings.

SERVES 8

FOR THE LEMON MAYONNAISE

1 garlic clove, peeled

1 pinch kosher salt

2 egg yolks

½ cup vegetable oil

½ cup olive oil

1 teaspoon lemon juice

FOR THE CHIVE BLOSSOM FRITTERS

8 cups canola oil

2 egg whites

1 cup sparkling white wine or beer

1 cup all-purpose flour

sea salt to finish

24 chive blossoms

TO MAKE THE LEMON MAYONNAISE In a heavy mortar, mash the garlic clove and salt into a fine paste. Add the egg yolks and, working the pestle in a circular motion, beat them until their yellow color begins to lighten. Combine the vegetable oil and olive oil in a liquid measuring cup or a vessel with a spout. Add the oil steadily, one drop at a time, while constantly moving the pestle around. If you are too fast, you will create heat, an enemy of mayonnaise. Once the yolks and the oil have formed an emulsion, you can pour the oil at a stronger pace, still moving the pestle. If it starts to look like it is about to separate, stop! Place the mixture in the refrigerator for 5 minutes. You can also sprinkle very cold water on the mayonnaise, which will help bring it together. After you have incorporated all the oil, add the lemon juice and give the mayonnaise a quick stir. Store in the refrigerator until you are ready to use.

TO MAKE THE CHIVE BLOSSOM FRITTERS In a medium saucepan, heat the canola oil to 350°F. In a medium bowl, beat the egg whites to form soft peaks. Whisk in the sparkling wine or beer, flour, and salt to taste. Dip the flowers in the batter and coat evenly. Gently place the flowers in oil and fry until golden, about 3 minutes. Work in batches of six at a time; do not crowd the pan. Remove the fritters from the oil and place them on paper towels. Sprinkle with salt immediately.

When the fritters have cooled slightly, gently move them to a lovely little platter and serve with lemon mayonnaise.

KEY TO
FRYING IN OIL

When you are about to fry anything, the first item you put in the oil is an experiment to test the temperature and see if the heat needs to be adjusted. It is similar to cooking the first pancake on a griddle. If the chive flowers brown too quickly, it's because the oil is too hot. Flowers are delicate and need a gentle fry, unlike a more robust item, like a potato.

Grilled Asparagus
with Farm Eggs and Grated Hard, Salty Cheese

Whether prepared on the grill or in a cast-iron skillet, this simple dish embodies spring. Let the heat from the asparagus melt the finely grated cheese. The yolk of the egg acts as a dressing.

SERVES 8

3 tablespoons olive oil

32 asparagus spears
    (about 2 bunches)

kosher salt

fresh ground pepper

6 sprigs tarragon, leaves
    removed from stems and
    stems discarded

½ lemon

8 farm eggs

½ cup finely grated hard,
    salty cheese (such as
    pecorino, Parmesan, or
    an aged goat cheese)

sea salt

Heat a large cast-iron pan or a grill on high. Add 2 tablespoons of the olive oil to the pan or, if using a grill, toss asparagus in 3 tablespoons of oil and generously season with salt and pepper. Transfer half the spears onto the grill or into the cast-iron pan. Roll them over after they acquire grill marks, about 4 minutes. Let them cook on the other side for no more than 1 to 2 minutes. Remove when slightly underdone. Prepare the second batch the same way, adding the remaining tablespoon of oil to the cast-iron pan if you are not grilling. Once the asparagus spears are done, toss them with the tarragon leaves and a good squeeze of the lemon.

Place eggs in a medium saucepan and cover with cold water. Bring the water to a boil and let boil on high for 2 to 3 minutes. Transfer the eggs to a cold-water bath or simply run cold water over them in the pan, displacing the hot water. Gently peel. Set aside.

To serve, pile the asparagus on a large platter. Carefully slice the eggs in half and place them around the outside of the asparagus, yolk sides up. Sprinkle grated cheese on top of the asparagus, then sprinkle the egg yolks with sea salt. Serve family-style.

Baby Beets and Beet Greens
with Fried Garlic and Chèvre

Young root vegetables with small, tender greens should be considered whole ingredients. The greens are treated differently from their roots, but they are just as edible. Clean them thoroughly and cook them just enough to wilt them. At this young stage, their flavor is earthy and sweet.

SERVES 8

a mix of small, colorful beets
   and their greens (about
   12 small or 6 medium
   beets)
3 tablespoons olive oil
1 splash red wine vinegar
1 garlic head, cloves
   separated and peeled
½ cup fresh chèvre
kosher salt
fresh ground pepper
sea salt to finish

Preheat the oven to 400°F. Separate the beets from their greens and wash the greens, then cut them into 2-inch lengths. In a large baking dish, combine the beets, 1 tablespoon of the olive oil, the red wine vinegar, and an inch of water. Cover with aluminum foil and bake for 35 to 45 minutes, or until fork-tender. Peel beets under cold water, discarding the peel, and slice into wedges.

Remove root ends of garlic cloves and slice cloves very thinly. In a large cast-iron pan, slowly heat the remaining olive oil over medium heat. Add garlic slices and fry until they are golden but not brown. Add the beet greens and turn off the heat. The residual heat from the pan will wilt the greens.

On a platter, lay down the beet greens and the garlic and arrange the beet wedges over the top. Season to taste with sea salt. Garnish with pinches of fresh chèvre, allowing the heat from the beets to melt the cheese.

Grilled Spring Lamb and Salsa Verde
with Smashed Potatoes and Alfonso Olive Tapenade

Grilling a whole lamb has become somewhat of a Memorial Day tradition for a big gathering at the farm, but here, instead we feed eight using lamb loin chops, which must not be cooked past medium rare! Following Argentine tradition, the meat is served with bright salsa verde, showing off an abundance of spring herbs.

SERVES 8

8 thick lamb loin chops

olive oil for brushing

2 cloves garlic, smashed and peels removed

1 pinch kosher salt

6 anchovy fillets

1 bunch Italian flat-leaf parsley, leaves picked from stems and stems discarded

6 sprigs mint, leaves picked from stems and stems discarded

6 sprigs tarragon, leaves picked from stems and stems discarded

2 tablespoons capers

zest of 1 lemon

juice of ½ lemon

2 tablespoons red wine vinegar

¼ teaspoon red pepper flakes

½ cup olive oil

Season the lamb chops with salt and pepper and brush them with olive oil. Let sit at room temperature for about 20 minutes.

In the meantime, make the salsa verde: In a small food processor, chop the garlic cloves with a pinch of salt. Add the anchovies, parsley, mint, tarragon, capers, lemon zest, lemon juice, red wine vinegar, red pepper flakes, and olive oil. Pulse until coarse, then taste. If it's too acidic, add a touch of olive oil. If it's not acidic enough, add a touch more lemon juice and red wine vinegar.

Get your grill going nice and hot. Cook the lamb until it has grill marks on one side, 6 to 8 minutes. Turn the chops and achieve grill marks on the flip side, another 2 to 3 minutes. (If you are cooking indoors, place a cast-iron pan over high heat for 3 to 4 minutes before introducing the lamb. Sear the meat until it's golden brown, then flip it and cook for another 4 to 5 minutes.) Do not overcook the lamb. When you press the meat, it should be soft in the center. Remove from the grill and let rest for 5 to 10 minutes. Drizzle the lamb with salsa verde and serve with smashed potatoes (see recipe on next page).

SMASHED POTATOES
AND ALFONSO OLIVE TAPENADE

Credit must be given to Francis Mallmann and his book *Seven Fires: Grilling the Argentine Way* for inspiring this recipe. Like a cross between a boiled potato and a French fry, this dish satisfies any potato craving. And your guests will love the unconventional presentation.

SERVES 8

6 medium Yukon Gold
   potatoes

6 sprigs Italian flat-leaf
   parsley, leaves picked
   from stems and stems
   discarded

2 tablespoons capers

1 cup pitted Alfonso or
   Kalamata olives

4 sprigs thyme, leaves
   removed from stems and
   stems discarded

juice of ½ lemon

zest of 1 lemon

¼ teaspoon red pepper
   flakes

kosher salt

fresh ground pepper

½ cup olive oil, plus more
   for frying

1 bunch chives, chopped

Fill a large pot with heavily salted water. Place whole potatoes in the water and bring to a boil. Cook until fork-tender, 10 to 12 minutes. Remove the potatoes from the water with a slotted spoon and let cool.

In the meantime, make the tapenade: In a food processor, chop the parsley, capers, olives, and thyme. Add lemon juice, lemon zest, red pepper flakes, ½ cup of olive oil, salt, and pepper and process until semi-smooth. A little coarseness is good. Taste and adjust seasoning.

Heat a generous amount of olive oil in a large cast-iron pan for a couple of minutes over medium heat. The oil should be quite hot. Slice potatoes in half and crush them, flesh side down, with your hands, allowing the skin of the potato to contain the flesh so they remain in one piece. Place 6 potato halves in the frying pan and fry until the undersides are golden brown. Turn with a spatula and brown the other sides. Transfer to a platter. Add a bit more olive oil to the pan and fry the second batch, then transfer to the platter. Drizzle the potatoes with the tapenade and sprinkle with chives. Serve family-style.

Rhubarb Galette

with Hazelnut Crust and Vanilla Ice Cream

A galette is a simple variation on a pie. It requires just one crust and is perfect for groups of six, but it can be stretched to serve eight. This recipe calls for ground hazelnuts in the crust, but ground almonds or walnuts would also be delicious. When making a galette, do not overfill the crust, as it will leak and become difficult to manage.

)

SERVES 8

FOR THE CRUST

1¼ cups all-purpose flour

¾ cup finely ground hazelnuts

¼ teaspoon kosher salt

12 tablespoons cold unsalted butter

1 to 2 tablespoons cold cream

FOR THE FILLING

3 cups rhubarb (4 or 5 stalks), chopped into ½-inch pieces

1 cup sugar

1½ tablespoons cornstarch

1 teaspoon vanilla extract

FOR THE EGG WASH

1 egg

1 tablespoon cream

2 tablespoons butter, melted

Preheat the oven to 375°F. In a medium mixing bowl, combine flour, hazelnuts, and salt. Work cold butter into the dry ingredients with your fingers until the mixture resembles coarse meal. Add just enough cream to bring the dough together. Form into a ball, wrap in plastic, and let rest in the refrigerator for 20 minutes.

In another medium mixing bowl, combine the rhubarb, sugar, cornstarch, and vanilla extract and let sit for 20 minutes, until the rhubarb releases its juices.

Between two pieces of parchment paper, roll out the chilled galette dough into a 9- to 10-inch round, large enough to reach the long edges of a rectangular sheet pan. Peel away the top sheet of parchment and place the bottom piece with the dough to your sheet pan, paper side down. With a slotted spoon, pile the rhubarb in the center of the dough and push it out to the sides, leaving about 1½ inches of dough around the edges.

Transfer the remaining rhubarb juice into a small saucepan and over medium-high heat reduce the liquid to about 4 tablespoons. The resulting syrup should be thick and sticky. Turn off the heat and let stand.

Use the parchment paper to pull the dough up and over the rhubarb, folding it over the filling. Repeat all around the galette, pressing the dough into the previous fold where it overlaps to prevent leakage.

In a small bowl, whisk together the egg, cream, and melted butter. Brush the crust with the egg-wash mixture. Bake the galette for 30 minutes, turning the pan after 15 minutes. About 10 minutes before the end of the bake time, pour the reduction syrup over the filling.

Remove the galette from the oven when the crust is golden brown and let it cool for 10 to 15 minutes. Serve warm with vanilla ice cream (see recipe on p. 113).

VANILLA ICE CREAM

You can make ice cream well ahead of your meal. Whenever I have an afternoon or an evening free, I'll make a quart of ice cream to be enjoyed later. This recipe is versatile and can serve as the base for many inspired flavors. Your eggs and dairy products must be as fresh as possible. Fresh eggs with deep orange yolks make for a beautiful and rich ice cream. And here's a tip: don't buy an expensive ice cream machine. A simple one will do, such as a Cuisinart 2-quart ice cream maker.

MAKES 1 QUART

1 vanilla bean

2 cups heavy cream

1 cup whole milk

1 cup sugar

1 pinch kosher salt

6 egg yolks

Slice the vanilla bean in half lengthwise, scrape out the insides with the blunt edge of a knife, and let rest on the knife blade, reserving the pod. In a mixing bowl, break up the egg yolks with a whisk. In a heavy-bottomed saucepan, combine the cream, milk, sugar, and salt. Warm over medium heat, stirring until the sugar dissolves; do not allow it to boil. Gradually ladle about a third of the warm milk and cream into the egg yolks, whisking constantly. Slowly pour the egg mixture back into the saucepan, stirring continuously. This is called "tempering," and it prevents the eggs from scrambling. Add the vanilla bean pod and seeds to the saucepan.

Cook over medium-low heat, stirring constantly, until the base thickens and coats the back of your stirring spoon, 6 to 8 minutes. Remove from heat and allow to cool while the vanilla bean pod steeps. Strain the base through a fine sieve into a glass bowl, cover it, and place in the refrigerator overnight. Make sure that your ice cream bowl and all its parts are in the coldest part of your freezer.

The next day, pour the base into the ice cream maker and churn according to manufacturer's instructions. Once it reaches a consistency you like, remove with a spatula to a quart-size lidded container and freeze for 30 minutes to 1 hour. Serve.

JUNE

•

THE FULL

STRAWBERRY MOON

The month of June is when lu-
pines, in their bright shades of
pink, purple, and white, flower
and unfurl; when peonies release their
tight-headed buds into billowy blossoms; and when strawberries ripen on
their vines, ready for harvest. June's full
moon is also called the Full Rose Moon,
the name a paean to the season's abundance of roses in all colors, shapes, sizes,
and fragrances. If rose petals are harvested at their peak, you can use them to
make a spectacularly scented rose water,
syrups, and so much more.

In June our farmers' markets are
finally flush with fruits, vegetables, and
flowers, and our gardens are reaching
maturity. The longest days of the year
have arrived, and we will relish every
last moment of daylight, whether floating about in the lake or sipping cocktails
with friends on the patio. This is what
we have all been waiting for: sweet summertime.

A wealth of perennial growth in June
calls us to spend time in the kitchen, preserving the flavors of early summer. We
make syrups of lovage, elderflower, and

rhubarb for cocktails and early-season
strawberry and rhubarb jams for desserts. Overzealous herbs such as chives
and tarragon are rolled into compound
butters and stored in the freezer for later
use. In the garden, Japanese beetles
munch tender greens into latticework;
the leaves are still rich in nutrients and
flavor and make wonderful pestos and
salsa verdes.

The June Full Moon Supper menu is
one that I look forward to for months.
I never tire of the rock crab salad with
minced cucumbers and flecks of tarragon on little buttered toasts, nor do
guests. A version of pasta primavera
tucks much of the season in between
ribbons of eggy pappardelle with decadent amounts of pecorino. A simple
salad of spinach and arugula shelters
baby carrot thinnings. And fat, bone-in
halibut steaks are cooked to moist perfection and served beside new potatoes
tossed in chive butter. Finally, we pay
homage to the moon's name with a
strawberry shortcake made elegant with
elderflower cream.

JUNE

•

FULL MOON SUPPER

MENU

Elderflower Martini
117

Buttered Toasts and Local Crab
with Chive Mayonnaise,
Cucumbers, and Tarragon
119

Pappardelle, Asparagus, and
Fava Greens
with Pecorino and Pea Shoots
120

Spinach, Arugula, and
Carrot Thinnings
with Sunshine Vinaigrette
123

Cast-Iron Halibut Steaks
with Herbed Compound Butter,
Radishes, Arugula, and Peas
124

New Potatoes
with Chive Butter
127

Cornmeal Shortcakes and
Early Season Strawberries
with Elderflower Whipped Cream
128

Elderflower Martini

While elderflowers grow in many rural places, they are difficult to come by in urban areas. If you can get your hands on a basketful of blossoms, steep the cleaned flowers in a quart of hot simple syrup for 2 to 3 days and then strain them out and bottle the liquid. The flowers are subtle in taste and take a while to impart their flavor to the syrup. Alternatively, you can use St-Germain, an elderflower liqueur that can be found at most liquor stores.

SERVES 1

1½ ounces vodka

½ ounce homemade elder-
   flower syrup or
   St-Germain

champagne topper

Fill a bar glass to the top with ice and add vodka and elderflower syrup. Stir with a spoon and strain into a chilled coupe glass. Top with a small pour of champagne.

Buttered Toasts and Local Crab
with Chive Mayonnaise, Cucumbers, and Tarragon

Crab toasts have gotten more mileage in my repertoire than just about any other dish. Something about the tang of the lemon zest, the crunch of the cucumber, the fresh medley of herbs, and the big pieces of soft, fresh crabmeat makes people swoon—and beg for the recipe.

SERVES 8

12 ounces fresh crabmeat, picked over for shell bits

1 small cucumber, peeled, seeded, and finely chopped

1 bunch chives or chervil, leaves picked from stems and finely chopped, stems discarded, plus more for garnish, cut into 2-inch pieces

1 bunch tarragon, leaves picked from stems and finely chopped, stems discarded

zest and juice of 1 lemon

2 tablespoons mayonnaise

1 teaspoon whole grain mustard

kosher salt

fresh ground pepper

1 sourdough baguette

melted butter for brushing

In a bowl, combine the crabmeat, cucumber, chives or chervil, tarragon, lemon zest and juice, mayonnaise, and mustard. Season with salt and pepper to taste.

Preheat the oven to 375°F. Slice bread thinly, brush one side of each slice with melted butter, and toast in the oven until golden, about 5 or 6 minutes.

Serve crab salad on toasts and garnish with chervil or chives.

Pappardelle, Asparagus, and Fava Greens
with Pecorino and Pea Shoots

Pappardelle is a long, luxurious pasta noodle that can be gently folded into a variety of ingredients. This dish is a sort of pasta primavera, taking advantage of proliferating asparagus, colorful pea shoots and flowers, and tender fava greens. In warmer climates, this dish could be made with peas and fava beans, which might be in season in June.

SERVES 8

2 tablespoons butter

2 sweet onions, peeled and diced

1 head garlic, peeled and minced

sea salt

1 bunch asparagus spears cut into 1½-inch lengths

1½ pounds pappardelle

2 tablespoons olive oil, plus a good pour

1 cup finely grated pecorino

1 cup pea shoots

2 cups loosely packed fava greens

zest of 1 small lemon

1 small bunch chives, finely chopped

fresh ground pepper

In a large sauté pan, melt the butter and gently sauté the onions and garlic in it with a generous pinch of salt until the aromatics turn soft and the onions are translucent. Add the asparagus and turn the heat up to medium high. Cook, stirring, until the spears turn bright green, and then turn off the heat.

Bring a large pot of well-salted water to a boil. Add the pasta and cook until al dente, about 5 minutes. When the pasta is just about finished, turn the heat under the asparagus up to medium and add a couple of tablespoons of olive oil. Once the pasta is cooked, drain the noodles, reserving 2 cups of pasta liquid. Add the liquid and the pasta to the large sauté pan with the asparagus. Add the pecorino and, using tongs, turn all the ingredients until well incorporated. Add the pea shoots, fava greens, lemon zest, and chives. Give them a few more turns. Season with sea salt and fresh ground pepper to taste. Serve warm with a good pour of olive oil.

Spinach, Arugula, and Carrot Thinnings
with Sunshine Vinaigrette

One of the glorious benefits of growing food is that a plant can be harvested at any number of stages. Carrots are the perfect example, as their seeds are so tiny that it is nearly impossible to space them out with precision. As a result, they grow in crowded rows and must be thinned. The dressing for this salad was named "Sunshine Vinaigrette" by one of my assistants, Rebecca, and its combination of sweet, acid, and aromatic flavors delights the palate.

SERVES 8

FOR THE DRESSING

2 garlic cloves, peeled

kosher salt

zest and juice of 1 lemon

zest and juice of 1 orange

2 tablespoons apple cider vinegar

1 tablespoon Dijon mustard

2 tablespoons honey

2 tablespoons minced lemon thyme

2 tablespoons minced lemon balm

1 tablespoon minced sorrel

fresh ground pepper

½ cup olive oil

FOR THE SALAD

2 cups young spinach, loosely packed

2 cups young arugula, loosely packed

1 large handful carrot thinnings (or thinly sliced carrots of various colors)

kosher salt

fresh ground pepper

To make the dressing, mash the garlic cloves and a pinch of salt together with a mortar and pestle. Add the lemon zest and juice, orange zest and juice, apple cider vinegar, Dijon mustard, honey, herbs, more salt, and pepper. Gradually whisk in olive oil. Let the flavors meld for 15 minutes before dressing the salad.

Wash the greens and carrot thinnings, dry thoroughly, and place in a big wooden bowl. Season with salt and pepper, then toss with some of the salad dressing. Serve the remaining dressing on the side in the mortar with a small ladle or spoon.

Cast-Iron Halibut Steaks

with Herbed Compound Butter, Radishes, Arugula, and Peas

By the end of June, in the garden peas hang heavily off their trellises and radishes have fattened up for the picking. While radishes are delicious sliced thinly and eaten raw, they are also fantastic sautéed with a little butter or roasted with olive oil and salt. Moreover, June is the end of halibut season, when fat steaks and fillets are full of flavor. Make sure to show off the whole golden brown halibut steaks before they are divided and smothered in homemade compound butter. Just about any herbs can be rolled into a butter—chives, lovage, sorrel, thyme, basil, rosemary, dill, or whatever else tickles your fancy.

SERVES 8

FOR THE COMPOUND BUTTER

16 tablespoons (2 sticks) unsalted butter, softened at room temperature

2 tablespoons minced chives

1 tablespoon minced sorrel

1 tablespoon minced thyme

1 tablespoon minced parsley

1 teaspoon kosher salt

sea salt for sprinkling

FOR THE HALIBUT

1 bunch radishes, tops removed

7 tablespoons unsalted butter

2 cups shelled English peas

2 large (or 4 small) halibut steaks (2½ to 3 pounds total), on the bone

fresh ground pepper

2 cups loosely packed arugula

1 squeeze of lemon juice

TO MAKE THE COMPOUND BUTTER In a medium bowl, gently mix butter, herbs, and kosher salt until blended. Press the mixture into a small crock and sprinkle with sea salt. Store in the fridge for use within the week or freeze for up to 6 months.

TO MAKE THE HALIBUT Slice radishes in half. In a medium pan, sauté them with 4 tablespoons of the butter and salt to taste over medium heat until they soften and begin to brown, about 5 minutes. Set aside.

Fill a medium saucepan with water, salt well, and bring to a boil. Pour peas into the water and cook on high heat until just tender, 2 to 3 minutes. While they cook, prepare an ice bath. With a slotted spoon, transfer the peas to the ice bath to shock them. Drain the peas.

Season halibut steaks with salt and pepper to taste. Melt the remaining 3 tablespoons of butter in a large cast-iron frying pan to coat the bottom. (For smaller steaks, you will need two pans, each with 1½ tablespoons of butter.) Place the halibut steaks in the pan and cook over medium heat until they are golden brown on the bottom, about 8 minutes. Gently flip with a fish spatula and cook for an additional 4 to 5 minutes. Be careful not to overcook.

In a medium bowl, toss the arugula with a pinch of sea salt and a squeeze of lemon. Arrange arugula on a platter. Take the halibut steaks and separate the

meat from the bone, then divide each half steak into two portions. Each steak should yield four portions (or two portions from each small steak). Array the halibut steaks over the arugula and put pats of compound butter atop the hot fish. Pour the peas and radishes on top. Serve family-style along with new potatoes with chive butter.

COOKING FISH ON THE BONE

While few Americans purchase whole fish anymore, options still exist for those interested. The halibut steak, which is a cross section of the fish, is sold on the bone and makes for a delicious meal. The bones of any animal have a good amount of collagen in them, lending moisture to the surrounding meat. It's critical that fish not be overcooked. You can cook fish two-thirds of the way through and trust that residual heat will finish the job. So often, home chefs will cook fish too long, to the point at which the flesh releases its proteins in the form of white matter. Once these proteins appear, the fish then proceeds to release liquid into the pan, the same moisture that is intended to stay in the fillet. It is this action that so frequently makes fish smell, well, fishy. If you are buying fresh fish and cooking it properly (not overcooking), your house should smell divine, not fishy.

New Potatoes
with Chive Butter

New potatoes come but once a year, and the best way to cook them is simply. Salt your water well so that the potatoes' taste comes through, and coat them liberally in butter and chives.

SERVES 8

25 new potatoes, scrubbed
　　and cut in half

1 large bunch chives, minced

8 tablespoons (1 stick)
　　butter

kosher salt

fresh ground pepper

Place potatoes in a large pot and cover with salted water. Bring to a boil and cook until tender, about 15 to 20 minutes. Drain. Toss potatoes with butter. Season with chives and add salt and pepper to taste. Serve in a bowl to accompany the halibut.

Cornmeal Shortcakes
and Early Season Strawberries
with Elderflower Whipped Cream

Born in the month of June, I insist on strawberry shortcake for my birthday dessert every year. The strawberry shortcake of my youth was made with store-bought angel food cake, Cool Whip, and conventional strawberries. Today, I bake homemade biscuits made of local cornmeal, slice up first-of-the-season strawberries from our patch, and whip fresh cream with a small pour of elder-flower syrup.

SERVES 8

FOR THE SHORTCAKES

1½ cups all-purpose flour

½ cup stone-ground
   cornmeal

1 tablespoon plus 1 teaspoon
   baking powder

¼ teaspoon kosher salt

¼ cup granulated sugar

4 tablespoons cold unsalted
   butter, cut into small
   cubes

1 cup heavy cream

4 tablespoons butter,
   melted, for brushing

2 tablespoons raw sugar for
   sprinkling

**FOR THE STRAWBERRIES
AND CREAM**

1 quart fresh strawberries

3 tablespoons sugar

2 cups heavy whipping
   cream

¼ teaspoon vanilla extract

1 tablespoon elderflower
   syrup or St-Germain

8 sprigs mint

Preheat the oven to 425°F. In a medium mixing bowl, whisk together the flour, cornmeal, baking powder, salt, and sugar until combined. Cut the butter into the dry ingredients till the mixture resembles coarse meal. Add the cream and stir until the dough comes together. Place the dough on a clean, floured work surface and form into a flattened ball or disk. Cut into 8 wedges and lay out on a sheet pan lined with parchment paper. Brush each biscuit with melted butter and sprinkle with raw sugar. Place in the fridge for 15 minutes to chill. Bake the biscuits until they are golden brown, 20 to 25 minutes.

Cut stems off strawberries and slice them in half. Sprinkle 2 tablespoons of the sugar over berries, stir a couple of times, and let macerate for 20 minutes.

In the bowl of a stand mixer, whip the cream together with the vanilla extract, the remaining 1 table-spoon of sugar, and the elderflower syrup until it forms soft peaks.

Slice each biscuit in half, like you would a hamburger bun. Place a spoonful of strawberries on the bottom half, then a spoonful of cream, then lean the top biscuit on the berries and cream. Garnish with a sprig of mint.

MAKING SYRUPS

There is no simpler way to preserve the scent and taste of spring and summer than making a syrup; sugar makes lovage, elderflowers, and rhubarb nearly immortal. Recipes for syrups generally follow the same principle. Make a simple syrup of equal parts water and sugar. Then the celebrated seasonal ingredient is usually cleaned, chopped up, and left to steep in the syrup for a while. Once the syrup is well infused, you strain and bottle it. It is now ready to use to flavor cocktails and desserts. Store in the fridge for up to six months.

JULY

•

THE FULL
HAY MOON

The July full moon goes by many a name—the Full Thunder Moon for the loud booms of thunder we hear during summer storms, the Full Buck Moon for the antlers that begin to push through the velvety heads of deer. But the natural phenomenon I most associate this month with is haying. Tractors move across the fields, rolling the long summer grass into huge bales. "Making hay" is a necessary prerequisite for feeding the cows come winter.

In the spirit of making preparations for the seasons ahead, we regard July as the beginning of the harvest, and as farmers and chefs, our minds turn toward the optimal use and preservation of food. Whether that means using an abundance of carrots to blend a carrot soup for twenty guests or packing beets, cucumbers, and beans into jars for the pantry, what to do with such a plentiful offering from the garden is an important consideration.

Activity at the farm ramps up in July, and the cooking school is busy with afternoon classes, week-long workshops, special events, and (of course) a July Full Moon Supper. This time of year, our guests come from across the country and beyond. They are delighted to be on the coast of Maine, experiencing the salt air on their skin, the sun on their faces, and glorious kitchen smells wafting out from the cooking school.

If planted at just the right time (not before the final spring frost and not too late into the summer season), cucumbers, zucchini, summer squash, and even cherry tomatoes will begin offering their first fruits in mid-July. But the most sublime July harvest of all are sweet, ripe berries. Throughout the state, one sees signs for Strawberry Festivals, Blueberry Wingdings, and Pie Competitions, all of which mark and celebrate the abundance of berries. An old-timer once told me that "back in the day," each town hosted a berry feast at the local grange hall, where tables were lined with bowls of berries and cream. For a small fee, little glass bowls were distributed to the guests, and they were encouraged to gorge themselves on berries and cream, as that would be their entire dinner.

Our July Full Moon Supper menu comes almost entirely from the garden, complete with edible flowers and generous herbs. Included in the harvest are delicate squash blossoms, brightly colored carrots, earthy beets, tender filet beans, sweet cherry tomatoes, and juicy raspberries. The dishes sing with color and flavor in a celebration of summertime opulence.

JULY

•

FULL MOON SUPPER
MENU

Negroni with Aperol
133

Fried Squash Blossoms
with Garlic and Parsley
134

Carrot Soup
with Pickled Beets, Fresh Ginger,
Greek Yogurt, and Fennel Fronds
137

Cherry Tomatoes, Green Filet
Beans, Chives, and Anise Hyssop
with Raspberry Vinaigrette
139

Locally Farmed Chickens
and Wheat Berries
with Grilled Baby Squash,
Tomatoes, and Summer Herbs
143

Raspberry Trifle
with Sweet Cream
146

Negroni with Aperol

A Negroni is a simple recipe to commit to memory: equal parts Aperol or Campari, gin, and sweet vermouth. The vermouth must be of high quality, as cheap vermouth makes for an overly sweet and cheap-tasting drink. Aperol is gentler that Campari, less bitter, a little sweeter, and floral. Its mild tones suit an easy, breezy summer afternoon.

SERVES 1

1 ounce Aperol or Campari

1 ounce Hendrick's gin

1 ounce good sweet
   vermouth (Cocchi
   Americano)

1 strip of orange peel

Fill a bar glass to the top with ice and add Aperol or Campari, gin, and sweet vermouth. Stir with a bar spoon and pour into a chilled lowball glass. Run the orange peel around the outside rim of the glass and drop it in the center of the drink.

Fried Squash Blossoms

with Garlic and Parsley

Some cooks like to stuff squash blossoms with goat cheese, shredded mozzarella, and herbs. I find that the flowers themselves are so delicate that they are best dipped in a thin batter and fried quickly alongside a little garlic and parsley.

SERVES 8 TO 10

4 cups olive oil or
    vegetable oil
1½ cups sparkling water
1 egg
1 cup plus 1 tablespoon flour
kosher salt
fresh ground pepper
4 cloves garlic, peeled and
    thinly sliced
8 sprigs parsley, leaves
    picked from stems and
    stems discarded
12 squash blossoms,
    stamens and bugs
    removed (see Note)

Heat the oil in a medium saucepan. In a medium bowl, whisk the sparkling water and egg into the flour to make a consistent batter. Season well with salt and pepper. Heat the oil until a deep-fry thermometer registers above 300°F, then add the garlic and parsley to the pan. When the garlic begins to brown and the parsley starts to shrivel and crisp up, use a slotted spoon to move them to a paper towel. Now you are ready to fry the flowers. Hold the squash blossoms by the stem and dip them into the batter, twisting them to cover the whole flower. Let the extra batter run off. Place 2 or 3 flowers at a time into the oil and cook until they are golden brown. You will need to turn them once for even cooking. Drain the flowers on the same paper towel and season again with salt after frying. Serve hot with bits of fried garlic and parsley.

NOTE It's no secret that little bugs live in flowers, especially flowers that have been recently harvested. Gently open each flower without ripping it and inspect the inside. Remove the stamen and shake any bugs outdoors.

Carrot Soup

with Pickled Beets, Fresh Ginger, Greek Yogurt, and Fennel Fronds

In July, the carrots that were planted in April and early May have some girth to them and are ready to be harvested. Depending on what color carrots you have (orange, red, yellow, or purple), your soup may take on a variety of shades. A garnish of pickled beets adds tartness, sweetness, and color to an otherwise monotone dish. As roasting and pickling beets is a fairly time-intensive process, make sure you start this dish several hours before guests are due to arrive.

)

SERVES 8

FOR THE PICKLED BEETS

4 medium red beets

1 cup red wine vinegar

1 small red onion, peeled and thinly sliced

1 bay leaf

1 garlic clove, peeled

6 black peppercorns

FOR THE VEGETABLE STOCK

1 yellow onion, peeled and roughly chopped

3 carrots, roughly chopped

3 celery ribs, roughly chopped

1 fennel bulb, stalk and heart removed, fronds reserved, and bulb roughly chopped

kosher salt

splash of olive oil

12 cups water

1 bay leaf

12 peppercorns

2 sprigs rosemary

2 sprigs thyme

2 sprigs parsley

continued on next page

TO MAKE THE PICKLED BEETS Preheat the oven to 400°F. Cut the greens and the root tails off the beets. Place the beets in a baking dish with an inch of water, cover with foil, and bake for 1 hour, or until fork-tender. Some beets are stubborn and will take longer. They must be fully cooked, but not to mush. Combine the red wine vinegar, onion slices, bay leaf, garlic, and peppercorns in a small saucepan to make the pickling liquid. Bring to a boil, then reduce to a simmer and cook until the onions soften a bit, 5 to 6 minutes.

Once the beets are cooked, peel them and slice them into small wedges. Slip them into the pickling liquid and let steep for a couple of hours.

TO MAKE THE VEGETABLE STOCK In a medium to large pot, combine the onion, carrots, celery, fennel, a pinch of kosher salt, and a splash of olive oil. Cover and sweat the vegetables until they are tender, 10 minutes or so. Add water, the bay leaf, peppercorns, and herbs. Bring to a boil and then reduce to a simmer. Cook for about 30 minutes. Strain the stock and set aside.

TO MAKE THE CARROT SOUP In a large, heavy-bottomed pot, combine the sweet onions, butter, and a pinch of salt. Cover and sweat the onions over medium-low heat until the onions are translucent and begin to break down without gaining any color, 10 to 12 minutes. Add the garlic, carrots, and ginger and cook, covered, for an additional 10 to 15 minutes, or until all the vegetables

FOR THE CARROT SOUP

4 sweet onions, peeled and
   cut into medium-size dice

4 tablespoons butter

kosher salt

4 garlic cloves, peeled and
   roughly chopped

5 pounds flavorful carrots,
   cut into ½-inch rounds

1 tablespoon minced ginger

8 cups vegetable stock

1 teaspoon red pepper flakes

kosher salt

fresh ground pepper

honey (optional)

FOR THE GARNISH

½ cup Greek yogurt

16 small fennel fronds,
   reserved from fennel bulb

good olive oil and sea salt

are tender. Add the vegetable stock and simmer for another 5 to 10 minutes. Using a blender, puree the soup in batches, tasting each batch and adjusting for salt, pepper, red pepper flakes, and sweetness. It's always better to taste as you go, as salt blended into the soup produces a rounder flavor than when it's added at the end. Add honey only if you think the soup needs sweetening; carrots are generally sweet enough on their own. Combine all the batches in a soup pot and let the flavors meld for at least a couple of hours before serving.

To serve, warm the soup over medium heat. Place 1½ ladles into each individual bowl. In the center, carefully lay 2 to 3 pickled beet wedges and a few red onion slices, being careful not to discolor the soup with the beet juice. Garnish with a dollop of Greek yogurt on top of the beets and a couple of wisps of fennel fronds. Drizzle a little olive oil around the outside of the beets and sprinkle with a touch of sea salt.

PUREED SOUPS

The beauty of pureed soups is their versatility. There is a soup for every season: an English pea soup or a lovage and lettuce soup in the spring, a corn soup with basil oil in the summer, a mushroom or squash soup in the fall, and a root vegetable soup in the winter. Their recipes are much the same: slow-cooked aromatics (such as onions, shallots, garlic, or leeks), the centerpiece vegetable, and stock or water. A pureed soup is dignified by a garnish that suggests the whole vegetable, such as a mushroom soup with sautéed mushrooms on top or a carrot soup topped with a colorful assortment of roasted baby carrots. Another option is using a natural complement as a garnish, such as a pureed pea soup topped with a few pullings of pink ham. Texture also factors into the presentation of a pureed soup; often, a crunchy buttered crouton can enhance an otherwise uniform meal.

Cherry Tomatoes, Green Filet Beans, Chives, and Anise Hyssop
with Raspberry Vinaigrette

Before the fat heirloom tomatoes are ready, cherry tomatoes, sweet as candy, ripen on their little green branches. Green beans hang by the hundreds on knee-high bushes. And my favorite herb, anise hyssop, is so full of sweet licorice flavor that it begs to be used not just in salads but in cocktails and desserts as well. The combination of fresh-picked herbs and flowers plus vegetables at their peak offers a vibrant and dynamic salad.

SERVES 8

FOR THE DRESSING

2 garlic cloves, skins and
    root ends removed

kosher salt

zest and juice of 1 lemon

1 tablespoon Dijon mustard

2 tablespoons raspberry
    vinegar

⅓ cup olive oil

fresh ground pepper

1 cup summer herbs, loosely
    packed (mix of basil, chives,
    anise hyssop, parsley,
    tarragon, and/or chervil,
    leaves picked from stems
    and stems discarded), chives
    roughly chopped and all
    other herbs left whole

FOR THE SALAD

2 pounds green filet beans
    (or other fresh beans, such
    as wax, green, or purple)

2 pints cherry tomatoes

borage flowers and anise
    hyssop flowers and leaves
    for garnish

TO MAKE THE DRESSING With a mortar and pestle, grind garlic cloves with a pinch of salt into a paste. Stir in lemon zest and juice with the pestle. Add Dijon mustard and raspberry vinegar and stir with the pestle for a minute or two. Stir in olive oil and salt and pepper to taste. Mince half of the herbs and mix them into the dressing. Let dressing sit for at least 20 minutes so the flavors meld.

TO MAKE THE SALAD Bring a large pot of salted water to a boil. Prepare an ice-water bath. Cook the beans in three batches, so as not to cool down the water too much. For each batch, boil beans just until they are tender, 3 to 4 minutes. Remove with a slotted spoon and then shock them in the ice water to halt the cooking process and so they retain their brilliant color. Cut the cherry tomatoes in half. In a large bowl, toss the tomatoes, beans, and the remaining herbs with the dressing. Add salt and pepper to taste. Garnish with edible borage and anise hyssop flowers.

EDIBLE FLOWERS

So often, when a flower is served as a garnish, the meal is eaten and the flower is left on the plate. The flower is a delicious extension of the plant and makes a tasty garnish. In extreme heat and sunlight, a vegetable flowers when it is going to seed, and often that flower—such as broccoli flowers and garlic scapes—tastes of the vegetable. There are many edible flowers you might never dream of putting in your mouth, such as sunflowers, daylilies (which are part of the onion family), calendulas, borage flowers, and sage flowers—which can add to the elegance of a dish.

Locally Farmed Chickens and Wheat Berries
with Grilled Baby Squash, Tomatoes, and Summer Herbs

While this chicken dish is well suited for summertime, it's a good basic recipe that you can adapt to any season. Cider and sage can dress it up for fall; spring onions, asparagus, and chives make it suitable for spring; and a spoonful of harissa and roasted winter squash enrich it for winter.

SERVES 8

¼ cup olive oil

1 large chicken, cut into
   8 pieces

kosher salt

fresh ground pepper

4 leeks, thinly sliced

1 onion, peeled and cut into
   medium-size dice

8 carrots, peeled and cut
   into 2-inch-long diagonal
   pieces

2 fennel bulbs, stalks and
   hearts removed and bulbs
   roughly chopped

10 garlic cloves, peeled,
   smashed, and roughly
   chopped

2 tablespoons flour

1 cup white wine

4 cups chicken stock

4 sprigs rosemary

4 sprigs thyme

2 bay leaves

1 lemon, sliced into rounds

1 bunch Italian flat-leaf
   parsley, leaves picked
   from stems and roughly
   chopped, stems discarded

Preheat the oven to 400°F. In a large Dutch oven, heat olive oil over medium-high heat for 2 to 3 minutes. Season the chicken pieces with salt and pepper and brown them in the pan, skin side down, about 5 minutes. Flip and brown on the other side, about 2 minutes. (If the chicken sticks to the pan, it is not ready to be flipped.) Remove from pan and let rest on a plate; the chicken will still be raw on the inside. Add the leeks, onion, carrots, fennel, and garlic to the Dutch oven and turn the heat down to medium. Add a touch of salt, cover, and sweat the vegetables until tender, about 10 minutes. Uncover, sprinkle the flour over the vegetables, and toss to coat them. Toast the flour for a minute or two, constantly stirring the contents of the Dutch oven. Stir in the wine, turn the heat up to high, and allow the alcohol to evaporate from the wine, about 5 minutes. Add the stock, rosemary, thyme, and bay leaves. Return the chicken to the Dutch oven and give the contents of the pot a stir. The stock should nearly cover the chicken. Turn off the burner. Top chicken with lemon slices. Transfer the Dutch oven into the preheated oven and bake until the chicken is golden brown and the liquid has thickened, about 35 to 40 minutes. Serve chicken over wheat berries and vegetables (see next page) with plenty of lemony sauce from the bottom of the pan and garnish with chopped parsley.

WHEAT BERRIES WITH GRILLED BABY SQUASH, TOMATOES, AND SUMMER HERBS

Wheat berries are one of my favorite grains to showcase in the summertime, particularly with grilled garden vegetables. The hearty texture of the grain stands up to the intensity of the charred flavor from the grill. Grains such as wheat berries, barley, and farro take about 45 minutes to fully cook in boiling water. Most grains should be served when they're a toothy, but not crunchy, texture.

SERVES 8

2 tablespoons butter

1 yellow onion, peeled and minced

kosher salt

4 garlic cloves, peeled and minced

1½ cups uncooked wheat berries

6 cups water or vegetable or chicken stock

3 tomatoes, cut in half

3 summer squash, sliced lengthwise into 3 or 4 pieces

2 tablespoons olive oil

handful of baby braising/ hearty greens (such as kale, Swiss chard, Asian greens, and/or mustard greens) or regular-size braising/hearty greens cut into thin ribbons

zest and juice of 1 lemon

handful of fresh herbs (sorrel, basil, parsley, lemon thyme, tarragon)

pinch red pepper flakes

fresh ground pepper

In a medium saucepan, melt the butter over medium-low heat. Add the onions and a pinch of salt and sweat them, covered, until they are translucent, about 10 to 15 minutes. Add the garlic and cook until soft, about 5 minutes. Add the wheat berries and toast them for about 2 minutes, stirring them around in the pan. Add the water or stock and bring to a boil. Give it all a stir and reduce to medium heat. Cover and simmer for 45 minutes, or until the wheat berries have absorbed all the liquid.

While the wheat berries are cooking, season and toss the tomato halves and the squash in olive oil. The following step can be done in a cast-iron pan or on top of the grill, using medium-high heat. Quickly sear or grill the squash pieces until they develop grill marks or turn a golden brown color, 4 minutes or so. Let them cool. Do the same with the tomatoes, about 3 minutes. Slice the tomatoes into wedges and the summer squash into bite-size pieces.

Once the wheat berries are fully cooked, turn off the heat and let them rest for 5 minutes uncovered. Toss the wheat berries with the greens, lemon zest and juice, fresh herbs, red pepper flakes, salt and pepper to taste, tomatoes, and grilled squash. Turn onto a large platter and top with chicken and sauce or serve separately.

WHOLE GRAINS

Some find it hard to get excited about whole grains. But consider this: It's a hot summer day, and pasta, polenta, and potatoes sound too filling. How about a grilled vegetable salad with a handful of herbs, a lemony vinaigrette, and a smattering of farro? Or a little wooden bowl of wheat berries, dried cherries, pistachios, and zucchini? Whole grains, which are common in many cuisines around the world, need to be more common in ours, replacing empty-caloried white carbohydrates. Heartier grains are often best served at room temperature, which means a meal can be made well ahead of time. Because they are quite filling and nutritious, just a cup of barley or wheat berries added to a salad will make it into a substantial meal. Digestion will be a lot smoother as well. So eat your grains!

Raspberry Trifle
with Sweet Cream

Nothing beats a trifle: gobs of flavored whipped cream layered with fruit and soft bits of cake moistened by alcohol. And so versatile! While a summer trifle is swollen with ripe berries and cream, a winter trifle can be layered with citrus and chocolate and Grand Marnier. And oh, how I love the presentation: layer upon layer of goodness, visible through a glass bowl, scooped in decadent messiness onto a plate.

SERVES 8

FOR THE CAKE

16 tablespoons (2 sticks)
   butter, plus 1 tablespoon,
   melted, for greasing
   the pan
1½ cups sugar
6 eggs
1 teaspoon vanilla extract
3 cups all-purpose flour
½ teaspoon kosher salt
2 teaspoons baking powder
½ cup milk

FOR THE REST

1 pint heavy whipping cream
½ teaspoon vanilla extract
1 ounce sherry
1 tablespoon sugar
2 pints raspberries
sprinkle of lavender flowers

TO MAKE THE CAKE Preheat the oven to 375°F. Grease a 12-by-9-inch cake pan with 1 tablespoon melted butter and dust with flour.

In a stand mixer fitted with the paddle attachment, whip the remaining butter. Gradually add the sugar, mixing until the butter becomes soft, light, and pale. Blend in the eggs one at a time, fully incorporating between each addition. Add the vanilla extract. In a medium bowl, combine flour, salt, and baking powder. Gradually stir the dry ingredients into the butter and egg batter, then stir in the milk. Scrape the sides of the bowl with a spatula a few times while mixing. Pour batter into the prepared cake pan and tap it against a counter to release any air bubbles. Bake for 25 minutes, or until a toothpick inserted in the center comes out clean; don't let the cake gain too much color. Let cool completely on a wire rack.

Just before assembling the trifle, in a stand mixer, whip the cream into soft peaks with the vanilla extract, sherry, and sugar. Using the mouth of a small mason jar or a cocktail glass, cut out circles of cake. This ensures the cake rounds will fit perfectly inside the jars in which you will build the trifle.

To assemble the trifle, layer raspberries, cream, and cake rounds in your glass vessel until filled. Garnish with a sprinkle of lavender flowers.

AUGUST

•

THE FULL
CORN MOON

August brings the highest temperatures of the year, and animals and humans alike spend hot afternoons cooling off in the abundant lakes and rivers across Maine. Down by the seashore at Salt Water Farm, the beach is covered in large rocks that absorb the sun's heat at low tide. When the tide rises, the rocks act as a natural water heater, tempering the ocean for a pleasant afternoon swim. The water is crystal clear, and you can see all the life on the ocean floor. These days are sweet and made sweeter by the knowledge that they are diminishing.

The August moon is called the Full Corn Moon, which signifies the bumper corn harvest that the summer heat delivers. When the first of the summer corn finds its way to market, we instinctively fill our shopping baskets. Back on the farm, we include corn in just about every dish: corn fritters, corn grits, creamed corn, stone-ground polenta. At Saturday's farmers' market, before I do a moment of shopping, I head straight for the corn muffins, made from home-grown, stone-ground sweet corn and tasting of pure sunshine.

The weather is usually dependable in August: clear blue skies and sun. Some crops have been waiting for the August heat to ripen them, such as many tomatoes, peppers, eggplants, and husk cherries; even the basil begins to bush out. Other crops, such as lettuces and legumes, either bolt or become woody and must be harvested and cleared out of the garden to make room for fall crops. Toward the end of August, blackberries finally debut, an official announcement that autumn is around the corner. The fields beyond the gardens gradually fade from vibrant greens to golden yellows, and the lupine pods dry out in the sun, soon to release their seeds back into the earth.

The August Full Moon Supper is an ode to the warmest, fullest, and most fruitful month of the year. Our menu pays homage to all that August brings: beautiful and fragrant wild mushrooms, sweet little cherry tomatoes, ripe peaches, and of course, late summer corn.

AUGUST

•

FULL MOON SUPPER
MENU

Pernod on Ice
151

Ricotta, Fava Beans,
and Arugula on Toast
153

Summer Mushrooms,
Stone-Ground Corn Grits, and
Fried Summer Savory
154

Heirloom Tomatoes,
Cucumbers, Maine Corn, and Basil
with Lemon Vinaigrette
157

Seared Cod
with Creamed Corn, Swiss Chard,
and Cherry Tomatoes
158

Peach Cake
with Mascarpone Cream
161

Pernod on Ice

Pernod is a legendary drink of writers and artists, one you rarely see outside of France. But that is no reason why we can't sip Pernod casually at home and imagine ourselves in a breezy café in Provence, the smell of lavender and olives in the warm air.

)

SERVES 1 ROOMFUL OF SOCIALITES

1 bottle Pernod
small pitcher of cold water

Set the bottle of Pernod on the table. Allow each guest a tall glass filled with ice, a teaspoon, and a chilled, empty short glass. Have people serve themselves, adding as much ice, Pernod, and water as they would like to their short glasses.

Ricotta, Fava Beans, and Arugula on Toast

This light snack pays homage to the fava bean, whose preparation requires a roomful of willing hands to shell and then shell again, all for the bright green, tender morsels within its furry pods. Consider enlisting your guests' help. While you can cook fava beans with the outer shell on, they won't turn out nearly as brilliantly colored as they will if you remove it.

)

SERVES 8

24 fava bean pods (or 1 cup shelled or frozen peas)

1 cup ricotta cheese

zest of 1 lemon

1 squeeze lemon juice

kosher salt

1 sourdough baguette

6 sprigs mint, leaves removed from stems and stems discarded

2 tablespoons butter, softened

sea salt

olive oil for drizzling

16 small arugula leaves (2 per toast)

Preheat the oven to 400°F. Shell fava beans, removing the pod, then the outer shell, then the peel if they've reached full maturity. Prepare an ice-water bath for blanching the favas, which will help them retain their brilliant green color. Bring a medium saucepan of well-salted water to a boil, add the fava beans, and boil until they are tender but still have a bit of resistance, no more than 2 to 3 minutes. With a slotted spoon, immediately transfer the beans to the ice-water bath. Once cold, drain them and set aside.

In a small bowl, prepare the ricotta by mixing in the lemon zest and a squeeze of lemon juice. Add kosher salt to taste.

Place the baguette in the oven for about 8 to 10 minutes, or until warmed through. Meanwhile, stack the mint leaves and cut in thin strips to make a chiffonade. Slice the baguette into ½-inch-thick rounds while still warm. Arrange slices on a large platter and spread with softened butter. Place a spoonful of ricotta on each slice, then a spoonful of fava beans. Sprinkle with sea salt and drizzle with olive oil. Garnish with arugula and the mint chiffonade.

Summer Mushrooms, Stone-Ground Corn Grits, and Fried Summer Savory

This dish is an opportunity to celebrate whichever mushrooms are in season, all on a bed of soft grits and with the simple accompaniment of butter, salt, and a handful of herbs. Top with a fried egg to make a breakfast fit for a king or queen. This dish also makes a wonderful, rich lunch on a winter day, prepared with dried and rehydrated mushrooms.

SERVES 8

8 cups water or chicken stock

2 cups stone-ground corn-meal (local, if available)

2 farm-fresh eggs

1 cup finely grated Parmesan

6 tablespoons butter, or more if necessary

kosher salt

fresh ground pepper

½ cup olive oil

8 sprigs summer savory

1 pound summer mushrooms (chanterelle, black trumpet, maitake, chestnut, lion's mane, or trumpet)

In a medium to large heavy-bottomed soup pot, bring the water or stock to a boil at high heat. Very slowly, shake the cornmeal into the liquid while whisking continuously to prevent clumping. Continue to do this until all the cornmeal has been worked into the stock or water. Turn the heat down to medium low and keep whisking until the grits no longer have a bite to them, 10 to 30 minutes. (Grits need constant attention.) If you are using packaged cornmeal, follow the instructions on the package.

Lightly whisk the eggs in a separate bowl. Slowly add a ladleful of grits into the eggs, whisking to incorporate. Add another and then a third, all the while whisking. Then slowly pour the eggy grits back into the pot, continuing to whisk the mixture. Allow the grits to cook for another 5 minutes or so while whisking constantly. The eggs will thicken the grits and make them richer in flavor. Add the Parmesan and 4 tablespoons of the butter. Once the butter and cheese melt, generously salt and pepper the grits to taste.

In a small saucepan, heat the olive oil over medium heat. Shallow-fry the savory sprigs 4 at a time. Drain on a paper towel and sprinkle with salt.

In a large frying pan, heat 2 tablespoons of butter over medium-high heat. Sauté the mushrooms in the butter, one handful at a time. Do not crowd the pan, as that will cause the mushrooms to sweat instead of brown. Resist the temptation to remove them from the pan too soon. When they are golden brown on one side, give the whole pan a toss and let them brown on the

other side. Transfer to a paper towel or a plate and salt them while they are hot. Continue sautéing the mushrooms in batches, adding butter as needed.

For each serving, place 1 large ladleful of grits in a shallow bowl. Top with a serving-spoon-size portion of mushrooms and then the fried summer savory. Serve warm.

Heirloom Tomatoes,
Cucumbers, Maine Corn, and Basil
with Lemon Vinaigrette

August is the month to showcase the many colorful varieties of heirloom tomatoes, perfectly ripe from the sun, served sliced and sprinkled with salt. A little sautéed corn, a few crunchy cucumbers, and a handful of basil leaves make this salad a fine tribute to the summer season.

SERVES 8

1 garlic clove, peeled

kosher salt

juice and zest of 1 lemon

1 tablespoon Dijon mustard

1 tablespoon local honey

2 tablespoons red wine
    vinegar

¼ cup plus 1 tablespoon
    olive oil

fresh ground pepper

3 small cucumbers

4 ears corn

4 heirloom tomatoes

petals of 2 small to
    medium sunflowers

2 bunches Genovese basil,
    leaves picked from stems
    and stems discarded

1 bunch purple basil, leaves
    picked from stems and
    stems discarded

With a mortar and pestle, grind the garlic clove with a pinch of salt. Add the lemon juice and zest, Dijon mustard, honey, and red wine vinegar. Mash the ingredients together with the pestle until incorporated. Stir in ¼ cup of the olive oil, and season with salt and pepper to taste. Let sit for 20 minutes to allow the flavors to meld.

With a vegetable peeler, peel every other strip of cucumber skin lengthwise, creating stripes. This allows the vegetable to retain a little color without overwhelming the salad with the bitterness of the peel. Slice the cucumbers in half lengthwise and remove the seeds if they are large. Place each half flat side down on the cutting board. Cut the cucumbers into ¼-inch strips lengthwise, then turn them 90 degrees and slice them every ¼ inch. The resulting pieces should be ¼-inch cubes. Place them in a medium bowl and toss with a small amount of the vinaigrette to make a quick pickle.

Husk the corn. With a sharp serrated knife, cut the kernels off the cobs. Heat a large cast-iron skillet over high heat. Add the remaining tablespoon of olive oil, the corn kernels, and a pinch of salt. Sauté the corn until golden brown on one side, about 4 minutes. Give the corn a stir and sauté for another 3 to 4 minutes, or until the kernels begin to gain color on the other side. Remove to a plate or platter and allow to cool.

Just before serving, slice the tomatoes into thick wedges. In a salad bowl, gently toss tomatoes with the cucumbers, corn, and a few spoonfuls of dressing. Garnish with sunflower petals and whole basil leaves. Top with sea salt and more dressing if desired.

Seared Cod

with Creamed Corn, Swiss Chard, and Cherry Tomatoes

In Maine, the season when we can make creamed corn with our own local sweet corn is brief. Cod, which is plentiful in the late summer months, has a meaty texture and pairs well with the decadence of this creamed vegetable. Cherry tomatoes are now extra sweet and, with a quick sauté and a handful of parsley leaves, make for the simplest of summer sauces.

SERVES 8

8 tablespoons (1 stick) butter

4 sweet onions, peeled and cut into medium-size dice

kosher salt

8 ears husked corn, kernels removed from cobs

1½ cups cream

fresh ground pepper

2⅓ pounds cod fillets

2 large bunches Swiss chard, stems removed and cut into ¼-inch pieces, leaves reserved

1 lemon

2 tablespoons olive oil

2 pints cherry tomatoes

1 bunch Italian flat-leaf parsley, leaves pulled from stems and stems discarded

sea salt

In a large sauté pan, melt 2 tablespoons of the butter over medium heat. Add half of the diced sweet onions and a pinch of salt. Sauté until onions are translucent. Add corn and another pinch of salt and turn the heat up to medium high. Sauté until the corn brightens in color, about 5 minutes, and then give the pan a flip and let the vegetables cook for another 5 minutes. Place half of the corn in a blender with the cream; add salt and pepper to taste. Blend until nearly smooth. Return corn purée to the sauté pan and stir to blend. The mixture should be soft, like a batter. If it's too dry, add a bit more cream. Season again to taste.

Preheat the oven to 400°F. Divide the cod into ⅓-pound portions. Salt the fillets generously. Heat two medium to large cast-iron frying pans over medium-high heat and place 2 tablespoons of butter in each. Sear the fish, four fillets at a time. Be careful not to crowd the pans, as cooking too many fillets will cause the fish to steam instead of gaining a crispy texture.

In a large frying pan, melt the remaining 2 tablespoons of butter over medium-low heat. Add the remaining diced onions and a pinch of salt, cover, and sweat the onions for about 10 minutes, until translucent. Stir in the Swiss chard stems and cook, uncovered, until they begin to soften, another 10 minutes. Slice the reserved Swiss chard leaves into 1-inch strips and then across the middle, so that no single piece is too long. Stir the Swiss chard leaves into the onions, turn the heat up to high, and cook until they begin to wilt, about 3 minutes. Add a squeeze of lemon juice if the vegetables become dry.

In a stainless-steel frying pan, heat the olive oil and add the cherry tomatoes. Sauté over medium-high heat until the first tomato pops. Give the pan a good shake to evenly distribute the heat among the tomatoes. Stir in the parsley, turn off the heat, and let the residual heat wilt the leaves.

To plate individual servings, lay down a bed of creamed corn, place a fish fillet on top, then use tongs to add a little nest of Swiss chard on the side. With a serving spoon, place a half-dozen tomatoes with parsley over the fish and chard, letting them roll around the plate. Sprinkle with sea salt and serve with either a squeeze of lemon juice or a lemon wedge.

FINISHING FISH IN THE OVEN

Fish continues to cook after it is removed from heat. Always take fish from the stovetop or the oven before it is fully done; otherwise, it will dry out. Depending on the thickness of the fish you are using, fish fillets may cook through on the stovetop, but if they are very thick, you may need to finish them off in the oven. You can tell by looking at its color how far up the flesh has cooked from its direct contact with the pan. If only the bottom third or half is cooked through, it will need to go into the oven for a couple of minutes.

Peach Cake
with Mascarpone Cream

Every August, at the Camden Farmers' Market, a lively couple sells peaches from a beautiful handwoven basket. If they are not all set aside for preorders, the peaches are gone in less than twenty minutes, as the townsfolk line up before the market opens to get their hands on them. It shows how rare peach trees are in Maine! This cake is the definition of comfort food. If you want an even richer crumb, use cream instead of milk.

SERVES 8

FOR THE CAKE

1 cup all-purpose flour

½ cup almond flour

½ teaspoon sea salt

2 teaspoons baking powder

9 tablespoons butter, softened at room temperature

1 heaping cup sugar

3 extra-large eggs

1 teaspoon vanilla extract

¾ cup cream

4 large, pitted peaches, thinly sliced

2 tablespoons melted butter

FOR THE CREAM

2 cups heavy cream

1 tablespoon sugar

½ teaspoon vanilla extract

½ cup mascarpone

confectioners' sugar for dusting

Preheat the oven to 375°F. Line the bottom of an 8-inch springform pan with a round of parchment paper. Butter and flour the sides of the pan.

In a medium bowl, combine the all-purpose flour, almond flour, salt, and baking powder. With a stand mixer fitted with the paddle attachment, whip together the butter and sugar. Incorporate the eggs into the butter and sugar one at a time, whipping well. Whip in the vanilla extract. Mix in a third of the dry ingredients, then a third of the cream. Continue alternating the dry ingredients and cream in thirds, scraping the sides of the bowl in between additions.

Pour the batter into the prepared cake pan. Spread the peach slices on top and press them into the dough. Brush with butter. Bake for 1 hour, or until the cake has set and turned golden on top. The cake is done when you insert a toothpick into the center and it comes out clean. Allow to cool on a rack or serve warm or at room temperature.

Using your stand mixer fitted with a whisk, whip the cream with the sugar and vanilla extract until soft peaks form. Fold in mascarpone.

Serve slices of cake on individual plates with a generous spoonful of cream and a dusting of confectioners' sugar on top.

SEPTEMBER

THE FULL
HARVEST MOON

The Full Moon Supper series was conceived on the night of a September Full Harvest Moon, a glowing red globe floating over the horizon. Traditionally, the harvest moon is a symbol of the season's hard work and its resulting cornucopia of food, a bounty for all species to enjoy. It's a time to be grateful, a time to preserve and ration for the long winter ahead, and a time to luxuriate in the final days of summer.

Even though bitter-cold days are still a couple of months off, we start to feel the change coming in our bones. The berries have dried on their branches; the tomatoes are so ripe they've split and are fit only for sauce. Heartier crops such as kale, carrots, chard, and Brussels sprouts, which have been waiting for colder nights, now take center stage.

The Maine woods are inviting in the early fall, their floors covered in roots, soft moss, and mushrooms of many varieties. September often brings rains from the Southern hurricane season, just enough moisture for black trumpets and chanterelles to begin popping up at the foots of trees and along wooded walkways.

September is the most abundant harvest month in Maine, in part because the August heat made vegetables grow exponentially, and you can bet that the garden holds some baseball-bat-size zucchini and summer squash. Blackberries grow thick along stone walls, and cucumbers seem to appear out of nowhere, a reminder that it's pickling season. Bush beans and pole beans offer the last new growth, basil is bushy and calling for an afternoon of pesto making, and in the orchard apple varieties are so crisp and flavorful that taking a bite is like the classic doctor's order.

There is no better time to be a home cook than fall. And, consequently, no better time for warm and rich soups, stews, and braises to reappear on menus—a slight solace for the impending cold. Cooks roll up their sleeves and turn to recipes requiring a few more steps and longer cooking times. Our homes fill with the smells of autumn foods: deep, rich, and complex dishes that call for our full attention.

SEPTEMBER

•

FULL MOON SUPPER

MENU

The Penicillin
165

Sheep's Milk Cheese
and Homemade Quince Jam
on Toasts
166

Queen of Smyrna Squash Soup
with Autumn Mushrooms
169

Fall Greens
with Irish Blue Cheese,
Roast Garlic Vinaigrette, and Apples
173

Red Wine Braised Chicken
with Chicken of the Woods,
Bacon, and Savory Herbs
174

Pear Tart Tatin
with Vanilla Ice Cream
178

The Penicillin

This is a good introductory drink for hesitant Scotch drinkers, as it tastes of much more than booze. Its name refers to its medicinal qualities, as it brings healthful honey and ginger into the mix—and it does, in fact, soothe a cold.

SERVES 1

FOR THE HONEY-GINGER SYRUP

2 cups honey

2 cups water

¼ cup peeled and roughly chopped ginger root

FOR THE COCKTAIL

2 ounces Dewar's Scotch

¾ ounce honey-ginger syrup

¾ ounce lemon juice

¼-ounce Talisker (or other higher-end Scotch) float

TO MAKE THE HONEY-GINGER SYRUP Combine the honey, water, and ginger in a small saucepan and bring to a simmer. Turn off the heat and let steep for 20 minutes, or until cool enough to place in the refrigerator to chill. Honey-ginger syrup will last for up to 1 month.

TO MAKE THE COCKTAIL Chill a rocks glass in the refrigerator. Fill a cocktail shaker to the top with ice. Add the Dewar's, honey-ginger syrup, and lemon juice, then cover and shake. Fill the rocks glass with ice and pour in the cocktail. Float the Talisker on top.

Sheep's Milk Cheese and Homemade Quince Jam on Toasts

Quince grows exceptionally well in Maine. It's a perennial fruit with beautiful coral flowers and makes for a nice medium-size plant in an herb garden or at the entrance of a vegetable garden. Quinces are hard as rocks when harvested and must be softened by cooking before you eat them. These days, you can find quinces in the tropical fruit section at most grocery stores.

SERVES 8

FOR THE QUINCE JAM

4 quinces

2 to 4 cups sugar

3 tablespoons lemon juice

FOR THE REST

½ pound Manchego or other
   sheep's milk cheese

1 loaf sourdough bread

honey for drizzling

Chop the quinces, unpeeled, into approximately 1-inch pieces, removing the cores. Place them in a large pot and cover with water. Bring the water to a simmer and cook the quince pieces until tender, about 30 to 40 minutes. Drain the fruit, then puree it in a food processor. With a spoon, push the puree through a fine sieve into a 4-cup liquid-measuring cup.

Measure the amount of quince puree and transfer into a heavy-bottomed pot. Measure out an equal amount of sugar—if you have 4 cups of quince, you'll need 4 cups of sugar—and add sugar to the pot, along with the lemon juice. Simmer for 1½ hours, or until the jam is an amber color. Pour into a couple of mason jars or crocks and let cool. Quince jam can be stored in the refrigerator for up to 1 month.

To serve, bring the quince jam and cheese to room temperature. Preheat the oven to 400°F. Warm the bread for 5 to 10 minutes, or until heated through. Cut into thick slices. Serve with cheese, quince jam, and a little pot of honey on the side.

Queen of Smyrna Squash Soup
with Autumn Mushrooms

While the Queen of Smyrna squash is easily found in our little corner of the world, any fragrant and colorful winter squash varieties would be a fine substitute, such as sunshine, butternut, or buttercup. Each squash has a different natural sugar content, so add a little honey to the soup if it's not sweet enough.

SERVES 8

FOR THE VEGETABLE STOCK

1 yellow onion, peeled and roughly chopped

3 carrots, roughly chopped

3 celery ribs, roughly chopped

1 fennel bulb, stalk and heart removed and bulb roughly chopped

splash of olive oil

kosher salt

12 cups water

1 bay leaf

12 peppercorns

2 sprigs rosemary

2 sprigs thyme

2 sprigs parsley

FOR THE SQUASH SOUP

1 Queen of Smyrna squash (or similar medium to large winter squash, such as sunshine, buttercup, or butternut)

2 tablespoons olive oil

4 garlic cloves, crushed with skins on

2 sprigs thyme, leaves removed from stems and stems discarded

continued on next page

TO MAKE THE VEGETABLE STOCK In a covered medium to large pot, sweat the onion, carrots, celery, and fennel with a splash of oil and a pinch of salt until the vegetables are tender, about 10 minutes. Add the water, bay leaf, peppercorns, and herbs. Bring to a boil, then reduce to a simmer. Cook uncovered for about 30 minutes. Strain.

TO MAKE THE SQUASH SOUP Preheat the oven to 400°F. Peel the squash with a vegetable peeler and cut in half. Scoop out the seeds with a large spoon. Cut the flesh into 1 inch cubes and set them on a baking sheet. Toss with the olive oil and salt and pepper to taste. Scatter the crushed garlic cloves and thyme leaves over top. Cover loosely with aluminum foil and bake for 20 minutes. Remove aluminum foil and let the squash brown for another 10 minutes. Squash should be soft throughout. You can test it by pushing a fork through the flesh.

In a heavy-bottomed soup pot, melt 2 tablespoons of the butter over medium-low heat, then add onions and a pinch of salt. Cover and sweat the onions for 15 minutes, or until translucent. Peel the skins from the roasted garlic. Add squash, peeled garlic cloves, and vegetable stock to the soup pot and bring to a simmer. Cover, turn the heat to low, and simmer for 10 minutes. Turn off heat. In a blender, puree the soup in batches, blending for 2 to 3 minutes at a time and adding salt, pepper, honey, and red pepper flakes to taste. (You will need honey only if the squash is not sweet enough for you.) If the soup looks too thin, don't use all of the

6 tablespoons butter

2 sweet onions, peeled and
cut into medium-size dice

4 cups vegetable stock

honey

red pepper flakes

½ pound seasonal
mushrooms (black
trumpets, chanterelles,
honey mushrooms, or
matsutakes)

liquid in the puree process. If it looks too thick, add more stock or water.

In a large sauté pan, melt 2 tablespoons of the butter over medium-high heat. Add half of the mushrooms and a pinch of salt, being careful not to crowd the pan, as this causes the mushrooms to lose their liquid. They will immediately absorb the butter, which will help them brown. Resist the urge to move them around in the pan. Turn them only once, when they have developed a golden brown color on the bottom, and sear on the other side. Move the cooked mushrooms to a plate and repeat the searing process with the second batch, using the remaining 2 tablespoons of butter and a pinch of salt.

To plate, ladle the soup into individual bowls and garnish with sautéed mushrooms.

PEELING SQUASH

If you are having difficulty removing the skin from squash, you can roast the squash whole in the oven, scoop out the seeds, then peel off the flesh. No need to do anything to it other than place it on a cookie sheet lined with parchment paper or foil and bake until you can easily stick a long, slender knife through the flesh, 45 to 50 minutes for a medium to large squash. Don't roast squash too close to the top of the oven, or the skin will burn and the flesh will dry out. You must let the squash cool substantially before you handle it.

Fall Greens

with Irish Blue Cheese, Roast Garlic Vinaigrette, and Apples

If we're lucky and the first frosts haven't devastated the last of the kale, mustard greens, and Asian greens in the garden, we make this salad as our last celebration of green for the season. A few crisp apples and a little decadent blue cheese make for a delightfully fresh and flavorful fall dish.

)

SERVES 8

½ cup walnut halves

1 head garlic

½ cup olive oil

kosher salt

1 tablespoon Dijon mustard

zest and juice of 1 lemon

1 sprig rosemary, leaves
removed from stems and
minced, stems discarded

2 sprigs thyme, leaves
removed from stems and
stems discarded

⅓ pound Irish blue cheese

6 loosely packed cups fall
greens (kale, arugula,
mustard greens, Asian
greens)

2 crisp apples (use sweet
and tart varieties such
as Honeycrisp, Cortland,
or Braeburn)

fresh ground pepper

Preheat the oven to 400°F. Toast the walnuts on a cookie sheet for 8 minutes. Place the head of garlic in a small baking dish; drizzle with ¼ cup of the olive oil and sprinkle with salt. Cover with aluminum foil and roast for about 25 minutes, or until all the cloves are soft. Let cool for a few minutes, then squeeze the garlic flesh out of the skins into a mortar. Using a pestle, grind the garlic together with a bit more salt. Mix in the Dijon mustard and the lemon zest and juice. Then add the rosemary and thyme and, using the pestle, mash to combine. Mix the remaining ¼ cup of oil and let the flavors meld for 20 minutes.

Slice the blue cheese with a vegetable peeler or a sharp knife. If the greens are quite large and not tender, chiffonade them by stacking the leaves and cutting them into small, thin ribbons. Just before serving, slice the apples thinly. Salt the greens. Mix the dressing and toss the greens with a few spoonfuls, just enough to flavor, not coat, them.

To serve, pile a tall nest of greens on each plate. Then place a few apple slices and cheese slices around the greens and sprinkle some walnuts on top. To finish, drizzle one more spoonful of dressing over each salad and give it a twist from the pepper mill.

Red Wine Braised Chicken
with Chicken of the Woods, Bacon, and Savory Herbs

Traditional coq au vin is made with old, tough birds (the wine and time spent in the oven tenderize the meat), but it can just as well be made with young, free-range birds. The dish is now a staple in the fall months at Salt Water Farm.

SERVES 8 TO 10

3 cups Burgundy red wine

1 teaspoon black peppercorns

3 peeled garlic cloves, 1 whole and 2 chopped

2 celery ribs, thinly sliced

1 medium carrot, thinly sliced

1 medium yellow onion, peeled and thinly sliced

one 5- to 6-pound chicken, cut into 10 pieces

8 sprigs Italian flat-leaf parsley

2 bay leaves

2 sprigs thyme

2 tablespoons olive oil

½ pound slab bacon, cut crosswise into ½-inch strips

2 tablespoons flour

2 cups chicken stock

2 shallots, peeled and chopped

kosher salt

fresh ground pepper

4 tablespoons butter

20 cipollini onions, peeled and quartered, or 3 yellow onions, peeled and cut into eighths

continued on p. 177

In a medium saucepan, bring the wine, peppercorns, whole garlic clove, celery, carrot, and yellow onion to a boil. Reduce the heat and simmer for 5 minutes. Let cool, then pour over chicken in a large bowl. Cover and marinate the chicken for several hours or overnight in the fridge.

Preheat the oven to 350°F. Tie the parsley, bay leaves, and thyme together with kitchen string; set aside. Remove the chicken from the marinade and pat dry with paper towels. Strain solids from the marinade and reserve both solids and liquid. In a large Dutch oven, heat 1 tablespoon of the olive oil over medium heat. Add bacon and fry until meat begins to crisp, 6 to 8 minutes. Using a slotted spoon, transfer bacon to a bowl. Increase heat to medium high. Working in two batches, brown chicken pieces for 6 to 8 minutes, flip them halfway through, then transfer to a plate. Add reserved marinade solids to the pot and cook until the vegetables are soft, 10 to 12 minutes. Sprinkle in flour and cook, stirring, for 1 minute. Whisk in the reserved marinade liquid, raise the heat to high, and bring to a boil. Lower the heat to medium and simmer for 5 minutes. Stir in the remaining garlic, chicken stock, shallots, and salt and pepper to taste. Nestle the chicken and herb bundle in vegetables. Cover and bake until the chicken is cooked through, about 1 hour.

While the chicken is baking, heat 1 tablespoon of the butter and the remaining olive oil in a skillet over medium heat. Add cipollini or remaining yellow onions and sauté until golden, 15 to 20 minutes. Combine the onions with bacon in bowl. Melt the remaining butter over medium-high heat, add mushrooms, and sauté until tender, 4 to 5 minutes.

1 pound mushrooms
   (creminis, oysters, chicken
   of the woods, and/or
   chanterelles), cut into
   quarters
1 tablespoon roughly
   chopped parsley

To serve, arrange chicken pieces on a large platter and top with sauce, bacon, onions, mushrooms, and chopped parsley. Serve family-style.

Pear Tart Tatin

with Vanilla Ice Cream

There is a bit of showmanship involved in making this dish, as flipping the pan requires a little faith. If you have properly caramelized the pears, the flip should leave just a few little pear bits behind, which can be removed with a spatula and carefully placed atop the tart. But the culinary theater doesn't end with the flip. This tart also calls for a technique called "flambé," or lighting alcohol on fire. If you are timid or don't have a gas stove, you can reduce the alcohol over high heat and skip the step involving flames. Also, when planning your supper remember that the ice cream needs to be made a day ahead of time.

)

SERVES 8

FOR THE PASTRY

1½ cups all-purpose flour

1 tablespoon sugar

½ teaspoon kosher salt

10 tablespoons unsalted
butter

ice water

FOR THE FILLING

4 Anjou or Bartlett pears

juice of 1 lemon

4 tablespoons butter

½ cup sugar

1 pinch ground cardamom

1 pinch cinnamon

2 tablespoons brandy

TO MAKE THE PASTRY Combine flour, sugar, and salt in a medium mixing bowl. Cut in butter until the mixture resembles coarse meal. Gradually add ice water 1 tablespoon at a time, until the dough comes together; make sure not to add too much water. Shape the dough into a ball, flatten into a disk, and wrap in plastic. Refrigerate the dough for 20 minutes.

TO MAKE THE FILLING Core the pears and cut them into thin slices and toss the pieces in the lemon juice. In a large cast-iron skillet, heat the butter, sugar, cardamom, and cinnamon until the mixture begins to caramelize, stirring occasionally. Turn the heat down to medium low, stir in the pears, and cook for 10 to 15 minutes, until they begin to soften and gain a bit of color. Add the brandy. To flambé the pears, tilt the pan toward the gas flame to light the alcohol. Lean away from the stovetop so you are not near the flame; it will subside in a couple of seconds. Let the alcohol evaporate off for a minute or two. Turn the heat off and remove the pan from the burner.

TO ASSEMBLE THE TART Preheat the oven to 375°F. Roll the pastry dough out between two pieces of parchment paper so it is the same diameter as the bottom of the skillet in which you cooked the pears. Lay the pastry round on top of the pears in the skillet, leaving the

caramelized liquid in the pan. Bake the tart for about
30 minutes, or until the top is golden brown. Let cool
for 10 minutes. Flip the tart onto a serving platter so
the pastry is now on the bottom. Slice like a pie and
serve each slice with vanilla ice cream (see recipe on
page 113).

OCTOBER

•

THE FULL

HUNTER'S MOON

October marks the transition into the cold and dark winter months. The instinct for survival becomes palpable. Small creatures put away reserves of nuts and berries, chickens are plucked from their coops by foxes at dusk, and hunters track through the woods in search of fat game for their freezers. After a frenzied summer season, October brings a welcome slowing down. Fall is a perfect time to reconnect with friends and family over shared feasts of slow-cooked dishes and cider.

Typically, the first half of October is a stream of spectacularly beautiful, crisp days as the foliage begins its colorful transition. Maple leaves turn brilliant scarlet, orange, and yellow; the oaks, russet; the aspens, pale yellow; and the poplars, golden. Of course, New England is famous for this change in the landscape, and to live here and bear witness to the symphony of color each year is to be royalty in our own land. Hikes up into the hills are a daily affair in the autumn, as every day truly feels like a gift. Many late-afternoon walks down leaf-covered paths evolve into a chance to share sundowners at someone's home, followed by an impromptu meal made from the late harvest.

October is particularly cherished by mushroom foragers, as it launches the annual hunt for the maitake, or "hen of the woods," a mushroom so prized in Japan that it is often given as a gift. It must be harvested at the perfect time, when it is still moist at the tips and full of flavor. Our mushroom-foraging friend claims that he harvests a gargantuan maitake each year from the same secret tree. When asked where this tree stands, he laughs and says, "Like I'd tell you!"

In our small community, there are at least a dozen families who raise pigs for the fall slaughter. Typically, butchering is done at the end of October or the beginning of November, when the air is nice and cool. Families with a chest freezer can store locally raised meat throughout the winter and into the spring. The best pigs are the ones fed on compost and fallen apples. A well-raised, well-fed pig has a far more complex flavor than commercially raised pork. We cherish our locally grown meat here in Maine and are grateful to those raising healthy and happy livestock.

With our pantries and freezers full and our orchards still flush with fruit, our October Full Moon Supper menu brings together a wealth of autumnal foods: slow-cooked white beans, foraged mushrooms, roasted pork loin, and sweet and tart apple pie. The sound of gunshots in the distant woods assures us that, indeed, the Full Hunter's Moon is upon us.

OCTOBER
·
FULL MOON SUPPER
MENU

Hard Cider
183

Chicken Liver Pâté on Toasts
with Apple Butter and
Red Onion Pickles
184

Great Northern White Bean Soup
with Oyster Mushrooms
and Sage Gremolata
187

Bibb Lettuces,
Caramelized Pears, and Hazelnuts
with Orange Dijon Vinaigrette
191

Bone-In Pork Chops
with Sage and Garlic Rub and
Braised Red Cabbage
192

Apple Pie
with Lattice Crust and
Maple Ice Cream
195

Hard Cider

So many delicious American hard ciders are available these days, many of them from New England. Seek out some of these new and likely unfamiliar labels and try them. Cider should taste of apples and be a bit sour from fermentation. The sweet mass-produced hard ciders will only give you a hangover.

)

SERVES 1

1 bottle locally made hard cider, not too sweet

Chill a tall glass. Fill with cider and serve.

Chicken Liver Pâté on Toasts
with Apple Butter and Red Onion Pickles

The sweetness from the apple butter and the pickled red onions balance the meatier flavor of the liver. To shorten your to-do list the day of the supper, you can make both the pickles and the pâté a day ahead of time, and their flavors will benefit from a day in the fridge.

)

SERVES 8

FOR THE PICKLED RED ONIONS

4 cups white vinegar

2 cups granulated sugar

1 cinnamon stick, broken up

4 whole cloves

2 pinches ground allspice

1 small dried chile de árbol

2 bay leaves

12 black peppercorns

4 red onions

FOR THE CHICKEN LIVER PÂTÉ

1 pound chicken livers

6 tablespoons butter

kosher salt

fresh ground pepper

3 shallots, peeled and
    minced

1 ounce Cognac or sherry

1 cup chicken stock

fresh ground pepper

1 tablespoon Dijon mustard

4 sprigs thyme, leaves
    picked from stems and
    stems discarded

zest of 1 lemon

continued on p. 186

TO MAKE THE PICKLED RED ONIONS In a medium saucepan, combine the vinegar, sugar, cinnamon stick pieces, cloves, allspice, chile, bay leaves, and peppercorns and bring to a boil. Peel the onions and cut them in half, then slice them about ¼ inch thick. Add the onions to the boiling brine and cook over medium heat for 3 to 4 minutes. Remove from heat and let them cool in the brine. Store them in a container big enough to allow the brine to cover them. They need at least 1 day to pickle and can be refrigerated for up to 3 weeks.

TO MAKE THE CHICKEN LIVER PÂTÉ Clean the chicken livers by washing them under cold water, then patting them dry with paper towels. Run your finger across the livers and remove any tough connective tissue between the lobes. In a stainless-steel or cast-iron frying pan, melt 2 tablespoons of the butter over medium-high heat. Season the chicken livers with salt and pepper. Add the livers to the butter in batches and sear on each side, 3 to 4 minutes on one side, then 1 to 2 minutes on the other; do not crowd the pan. Remove them and place onto a cutting board when they are rare to medium rare at the center, not a touch more. Slice into the meat to check for doneness. This ensures you will produce a beautifully pink pâté.

Using the same pan, sauté the shallots with a touch of salt over medium heat until soft, about 2 minutes, stirring occasionally. Turn off the heat, add the Cognac or sherry, and turn the heat back up to medium high. If you are using a gas stovetop, the liquor will ignite, especially if you tip the pan to expose the booze to the

1 batch homemade apple
    butter (see recipe below)
    or one 8-ounce jar apple
    butter

1 large, crusty loaf
    sourdough bread

flame, which adds to the flavor of the pâté. (Be very careful when cooking alcohol over a flame.) If you have an electric stovetop, skip this step of igniting the liquor.

Stir in the chicken stock, turn the heat up to high and add another pinch of salt and a grind of pepper. Once you have about 4 tablespoons of pan-sauce reduction, remove it from the heat and let it cool.

In a medium food processor, combine the chicken livers, reduction, Dijon mustard, thyme, remaining 4 tablespoons of butter, and lemon zest. Season with salt and pepper and pulse the pâté until it is uniformly smooth. Transfer to a small crock or ramekin and let it cool completely.

To serve, preheat the oven to 400°F. Warm the bread for 5 to 10 minutes. Remove and slice in half lengthwise, then cut into ½-inch-thick slices. Serve with the crock of chicken liver pâté, red onion pickles, and a little pot of apple butter.

APPLE BUTTER

Apple butter from scratch is a simple project, and your home will smell rich with autumn fruit for hours.

MAKES 8 OUNCES

4 pounds soft apples, such
    as Braeburn, Cortland, or
    McIntosh

2 to 3 tablespoons lemon
    juice (depending on
    tartness of apples)

2 cups water

½ cup sugar for every cup
    of apple pulp

1 cinnamon stick

Core the apples, chop them up into large chunks, and toss them in a large bowl with the lemon juice. There is no need to peel them, as the peel contains thickening agents that will be useful. Place the apple chunks in a large pot with the water. Bring to a boil, reduce to a simmer, and cook until the apples are tender, about 20 minutes. Strain the apples, discarding the liquid.

With a spoon, push the apples through a sieve. Measure out the pulp: for every cup of apple pulp, you will use ½ cup sugar. Combine apple pulp and sugar in a medium, thick-bottomed pot and toss in a cinnamon stick. Cook over low to medium-low heat for 1 to 2 hours, until the apple butter is thick (it will be spreadable once it cools). Taste for sweetness. Store in a glass mason jar. Apple butter will keep for up to 1 month in the refrigerator or can be frozen for up to 6 months.

Great Northern White Bean Soup

with Oyster Mushrooms and Sage Gremolata

Part of what makes a bean soup so enjoyable this time of year is the age-old tradition of shelling beans. Both the stock and the beans can be prepared a day or two ahead of the feast. As fall cooking is often rich and heavy, a gremolata offers a contrasting lightness and freshness while simultaneously packing a little punch. Gremolata is a mince traditionally made up of fresh parsley, lemon zest, and minced garlic. It is served atop the richest and creamiest of dishes, such as osso bucco. In this recipe, we slightly sauté the garlic in oil before combining it with sage and lemon zest to subdue the piquant flavor that raw garlic offers.

SERVES 8

FOR THE CHICKEN STOCK

1 yellow onion, roughly
    chopped
2 carrots, roughly chopped
    (including tops)
2 celery ribs, roughly
    chopped (including
    leaves)
kosher salt
1 chicken carcass
bouquet garni (2 sprigs
    thyme, 2 sprigs rosemary,
    2 sprigs parsley, 1 bay
    leaf, and 12 peppercorns)

FOR THE BEANS

3 cups dry Great Northern
    white beans or soldier
    beans
½ yellow onion, unpeeled
3 to 4 garlic cloves, unpeeled
1 bay leaf
3 sprigs thyme
2 tablespoons kosher salt

continued on next page

TO MAKE THE CHICKEN STOCK In a large stockpot, warm the olive oil and combine the onion, carrots, and celery with a touch of salt. Cover and sweat over medium-low heat until vegetables are softened. Place the chicken carcass in the pot and cover with water. Add the bouquet garni and bring to a boil, then reduce to a simmer. Cook for 1 hour. As the stock simmers, remove any foam that rises to the top with a slotted spoon. Strain the stock through a fine-mesh strainer. Use within 3 days or freeze for up to 6 months.

TO MAKE THE BEANS Soak the beans overnight. Rinse them under cold water, place them in a medium to large soup pot, and cover them with water. Toss in the onion, garlic, bay leaf, and thyme sprigs. Salt the water very generously with the kosher salt. Bring the pot to a high boil, and with a slotted spoon skim off the foam that rises to the top. Then reduce the heat to medium low and simmer gently for 1 to 1½ hours, or until the beans are tender. They should be soft but with some structural integrity. When you are tasting the beans for doneness, also taste for salt and add more if needed. Once the beans are cooked, drain and reserve them.

TO MAKE THE SAGE GREMOLATA In a small saucepan, sauté the garlic in olive oil over medium heat until it's soft and fragrant. Let cool. Add the sage to the oil and

FOR THE SAGE GREMOLATA

1 garlic clove, peeled and
minced

2 tablespoons olive oil

12 sage leaves, cut into
chiffonade

zest of 1 lemon

pinch sea salt

pinch red pepper flakes

good-quality olive oil

FOR THE SOUP

6 to 8 tablespoons unsalted
butter

2 large sweet onions, peeled
and cut into medium-size
dice

kosher salt

4 garlic cloves, peeled and
minced

8 cups homemade chicken
stock (see recipe above)

fresh ground pepper

red pepper flakes (optional)

1 pound maitake or oyster
mushrooms

good-quality olive oil for
drizzling

stir. Place the garlic-and-sage-infused oil in a little bowl with the lemon zest, sea salt, and red pepper flakes. Mix together and set aside.

TO MAKE THE SOUP In a medium to large, heavy-bottomed soup pot, melt 2 tablespoons of the butter over medium heat. Add sweet onions and a touch of salt, cover, then sweat the onions for 15 minutes, checking them every few minutes. Once they are translucent and tender, add the garlic and sweat, covered, for another 5 minutes. Add the beans to the pot, pour the chicken stock over them, bring to a simmer, and cook over medium heat for 5 minutes more.

In a blender or food processor, puree the soup in batches, adding just enough liquid and beans to each batch to get a consistency that is not too thick and not too thin. (It's perfectly fine to leave some stock behind rather than producing a soup that's too thin; it is hard to rethicken pureed soup.) Salt and pepper each batch to taste and add a pinch of red pepper flakes if you'd like. Rinse out your soup pot, and once you are finished blending, pour the soup back into the pot. Cover and set aside.

Slice the mushrooms into small pieces. In a large cast-iron frying pan, heat 2 tablespoons of butter over medium-high heat. Sear the mushrooms in batches, about 3 to 4 minutes on each side, making sure not to crowd the pan with more than one roomy layer. Salt the mushrooms in the pan while searing them and do not stir them around too much; let them get color on each side. As they are finished, transfer them to a platter. Sear each additional batch with another 2 tablespoons butter and additional salt.

To serve, warm the soup over medium-low heat. Taste again and add more salt and pepper as needed. If the soup has thickened, add a little stock or water. If desired, warm up the mushrooms over high heat for a couple of minutes. Pour 1½ ladlefuls of soup in each individual shallow soup bowl. Place a spoonful of mushrooms at the center of the soup and sprinkle sage gremolata on top. Drizzle good-quality olive oil over the soup to finish.

Bibb Lettuces, Caramelized Pears, and Hazelnuts

with Orange Dijon Vinaigrette

Pears sliced in half lengthwise, caramelized, and presented on a bed of delicate Bibb lettuce always delight the eye. A bright orange vinaigrette balances the sweetness of the fruit, and the hazelnuts give the dish an earthy undertone.

))

SERVES 8

2 heads Bibb lettuce

½ cup hazelnuts

1 garlic clove, peeled

1 tablespoon Dijon mustard

zest and juice of 1 orange

2 tablespoons sherry
   vinegar

kosher salt

fresh ground pepper

2 tablespoons hazelnut oil

¼ cup olive oil

4 semifirm pears, such as
   Anjou or Bartlett

2 tablespoons butter

2 tablespoons maple syrup

Preheat the oven to 375°F. Tear the Bibb lettuce leaves into large, bite-size pieces. Wash, dry, and chill in the refrigerator. On a sheet pan, toast the hazelnuts for 5 to 8 minutes.

In a mortar, pound the garlic clove and a pinch of salt with a pestle to make a garlic paste. Add the Dijon mustard, orange zest and juice, sherry vinegar, and salt and pepper to taste. Give the dressing a good stir. Add the hazelnut and olive oils and stir again. Set aside to let the flavors meld for 20 minutes.

Meanwhile, slice the pears in half lengthwise. Place them facedown in a large frying pan. Add the butter and the maple syrup and sauté over medium heat. Once the butter has melted, give the pan a shake or stir the pears around to make sure that they are not sticking. Cook them until they have a beautiful golden brown color. Watch the pears carefully, as they can caramelize quickly. If they are ripe, they will not need much more than 5 to 10 minutes of cooking time. When they are finished, let them cool or serve them warm.

Just before serving, season the Bibb lettuce with salt and toss with a couple of tablespoons of dressing. Arrange a nest of lettuce on each individual plate, set a pear beside it, and sprinkle with a few hazelnuts. Spoon a little more dressing over the top.

Bone-In Pork Chops
with Sage and Garlic Rub and Braised Red Cabbage

My dear dad, Lance, deserves some credit for this dish. He made it first for himself and my mother, then for friends, and finally, I asked him to make it for a Full Moon Supper. It's a wonderful combination of fall ingredients, and the pork tastes infinitely better cooked on the bone than off.

SERVES 8

FOR THE CABBAGE

2 tablespoons butter

2 sweet onions, peeled and thinly sliced

kosher salt

1 small red cabbage, cut into thin, ½-inch-long strips

2 cups apple cider

FOR THE PORK

1 garlic head, cloves peeled and roughly chopped, plus ½ garlic head, cloves separated and left in skins

2 tablespoons olive oil

12 fresh sage leaves, finely chopped

kosher salt

fresh ground pepper

1 bone-in pork loin roast with 8 ribs

2 pounds baby red potatoes

2 yellow onions, peeled and cut into wedges

4 tablespoons butter, melted

1 cup white wine

1 cup chicken stock or water

1½ pounds apples (use tart and sweet varieties such as Cortland, Honeycrisp, and Braeburn), cored and cut into wedges

TO MAKE THE CABBAGE Warm butter in a large, heavy-bottomed Dutch oven over medium heat. Add the sweet onions and a big pinch of salt, cover, and sweat the onions over medium-low heat for 15 to 20 minutes, until they are translucent and beginning to break down. Add the cabbage and a generous amount of salt. Add the cider, cover, turn the heat up to medium, and cook for 20 minutes, stirring from time to time. Uncover and cook for another 10 to 15 minutes, stirring occasionally. The cabbage should begin to break down but without losing its structure.

TO MAKE THE PORK Preheat the oven to 425°F. In a mortar, combine the peeled garlic, olive oil, and half of the chopped sage leaves. Rough the mixture up with a pestle for a few minutes. Salt and pepper the pork generously and rub it with the mashed garlic, sage, and olive oil. Cut the potatoes in half. Salt and pepper them generously. In a large bowl, toss the potatoes and the onions with the melted butter and the remaining chopped sage. Set the pork loin in the center of a large roasting pan and surround it with potatoes and onions. Tuck the separated, unpeeled garlic cloves into the onions and potatoes. Pour wine and stock over the vegetables and around the roast. Roast the pork for 20 minutes, until the outside begins to brown. Remove from the oven and toss the apple wedges in with the potatoes and a pinch each of salt and pepper. Return to the oven to roast for another 45 minutes, or until the temperature of the pork is 145°F. Remove from the oven and let rest for 15 minutes.

To serve, separate the ribs with a sharp carving

knife. On each plate, lay down a bed of cabbage and
top with a pork rib, a spoonful of apples, onions, and
potatoes, and a spoonful of drippings from the bottom
of the roasting pan.

Apple Pie
with Lattice Crust and Maple Ice Cream

Many guests at Salt Water Farm tell me they shy away from making pie crust at home. It's a pity, because there is nothing more satisfying than a beautiful pie baked from scratch—and a lattice crust never fails to impress. The maple ice cream should be prepared a day ahead.

**SERVES 8
(ONE 8-INCH PIE)**

FOR THE PIE CRUST

2½ cups flour, sifted

2 tablespoon sugar, plus
   more for sprinkling

1 teaspoon kosher salt

18 tablespoons cold
   unsalted butter, cut into
   small pieces

3 to 5 tablespoons ice water

FOR THE FILLING

5 to 6 apples, cored and
   thinly sliced (use tart and
   sweet varieties, like
   Braeburn or Honeycrisp)

¾ cup sugar

2 tablespoons cornstarch

2 tablespoons apple cider
   vinegar

1 teaspoon ground cinnamon

¼ teaspoon kosher salt

¼ teaspoon fresh ground
   nutmeg

1 egg, lightly beaten

1 tablespoon heavy cream

2 tablespoons melted butter

1 tablespoon raw sugar

TO SERVE

1 batch maple ice cream

TO MAKE THE MAPLE ICE CREAM Follow the recipe on page 113 for vanilla ice cream, substituting ½ cup of maple syrup and ½ cup of sugar for the 1 cup of sugar.

TO MAKE THE CRUST Whisk the flour, sugar, and salt in a medium mixing bowl. Cut in the butter until the mixture resembles coarse meal. Gradually mix in ice water, 1 tablespoon at a time, until the dough comes together. Transfer dough to a lightly floured surface, divide in half, and form 2 dough balls, one slightly bigger than the other. Flatten each ball slightly to make a disk. Wrap disks in plastic wrap and refrigerate for 20 minutes.

Preheat the oven to 425°F. Between two pieces of parchment paper, roll out the larger of the two disks to a thickness of about ⅛ inch. Line a 9-inch pie dish with the larger pastry and refrigerate for 15 minutes. Roll out the other disk between the same two pieces of parchment paper and place on a sheet pan in the refrigerator.

TO MAKE THE FILLING In a medium bowl, combine the apples, sugar, cornstarch, vinegar, cinnamon, salt, and nutmeg. Spoon the filling into the chilled bottom pie crust. Remove the top crust from the refrigerator and cut into six ½-inch-long strips. Lay three strips horizontally across the middle of the pie and fold the first and the third halfway back, left over right. Lay a fourth strip perpendicularly across the center and unfold the first and third strips over the fourth strip. Lay a fifth strip parallel and to the left of the fourth strip, over the first and third strips under the second strip. Pick up the right side of the second strip and lay a sixth strip over the first and third strips, parallel to the fourth and fifth strips. Lay the second strip back down on top of the sixth strip. Pinch the edge of the pie together where the strips meet and then crimp the edges all the way around.

Make an egg wash by whisking together the egg, cream, and melted butter in a small mixing bowl. Brush the pastry lattice with the egg wash and sprinkle with raw sugar. Bake the pie for 20 minutes. Reduce heat to 350°F and continue baking until the crust is golden brown, about 40 minutes more. Transfer the pie to a rack and cool for 2 hours before serving. (Cooling is essential, as all pies must set properly.) Once fully cooled and set, serve each slice with a scoop of maple ice cream.

THE FULL

BEAVER MOON

The November moon is named for a Native American tradition of setting beaver traps before the streams and rivers freeze, in pursuit of warm winter furs. It is also referred to as the First Frost Moon, but in Maine's upper regions, a frost can come well before November. With good planning and a northern sensibility, by November a chef has stocked the kitchen for the winter months and piled plenty of dry wood in the barn. The first forecasted snow brings mixed feelings of childish delight and dread: a reminder to turn inward, toward home and hearth.

November can be jarring to our systems: life slows to a near halt, fundamentally altering our routines. We must resist the urge to hibernate, and this is where communal cooking plays its valuable role. What better way to pass the long, dark hours than together with a few bottles of wine and many hands making light work of a beautiful meal? Dinnertime comes early on these short days so that we can go to sleep at a reasonable hour and wake up with the sun. But if spirits are high and the company is good, you might find yourself up long after bedtime, without regret.

Fire plays a part in our evening affairs, not only in keeping us warm but providing a source of light around which to gather and converse. Maine is so far east on our continent that the sun sets and the dark settles in over the coast by 4 P.M. We take great care to put the birds in before dusk, after which the fox and other predators are scouring the hills, looking for their own food stock for winter.

November is also the start of the holiday season, a festive call to friends and relatives to repose lazily around the table, putting grievances aside in the name of merriment and feast. Everyone brings a favorite dish or culinary tradition to weave into the meal, and a bounty of foods emerges on the buffet, made by a collection of hands and minds.

Our November Full Moon Supper menu is intended to be a bit decadent, as the holidays are cause for at least minor indulgence. We celebrate ingredients that are still fresh from the earth, such as potatoes, Brussels sprouts, and cranberries. Poultry plays an important role in the holiday season, and in lieu of turkey, we dine on rich duck breast surrounded by heirloom beans, which have been shelled and dried after ample time left hanging on their stalks in the barn. A chocolate cake finishes the meal, made light with almond flour and lavishly drizzled in crème anglaise. Meanwhile, the cold November winds carry the autumn leaves away, making space for imminent snowfall.

NOVEMBER

FULL MOON SUPPER

MENU

Remember the Maine
201

Oven Tart
with Sweet Onions, Pecorino,
Anchovies, Capers, and Lemon
203

Mussel Chowder
with Leeks and Heirloom Potatoes
204

Raw Brussels Sprouts
and Kale Salad
with Cranberries and Almonds
207

Duck Breast
with Jacob's Cattle Beans
and Roast Apples
208

Chocolate Almond Brandy Cake
with Crème Anglaise
211

Remember the *Maine*

While I like to think that this drink was named after the great state of Maine, it was actually named for a ship that went down during the Spanish-American War. It's stiff and delicious and will spark your appetite for the meal ahead.

)

SERVES 1

2 ounces Old Overholt rye

¾ ounce Cocchi Vermouth di Torino

½ ounce Cherry Heering

3 drops absinthe or Pernod

1 strip of orange peel

Fill a bar glass to the top with ice, then pour in rye, vermouth, Cherry Heering, and absinthe or Pernod. Stir with a bar spoon and strain into a chilled coupe glass. Bend the strip of orange peel in half and warm the skin side with the flame of a match. Then turn the inside of the peel toward the heat, squeeze the skin sides together to release the oils, and hold it up to the flame. The peel should ignite. Drop the flaming orange peel into the cocktail.

Oven Tart

with Sweet Onions, Pecorino, Anchovies, Capers, and Lemon

This recipe is inspired by a regional tart from Alsace-Lorraine in northeastern France called a "pissaladière," typically made with sweet onions, bacon, olives, and anchovies. I can't resist topping it with thinly sliced lemons, which crisp up in the oven and are wonderfully sweet and tart.

SERVES 8

FOR THE DOUGH

1 cup warm water

1½ teaspoons baker's yeast

2½ cups all-purpose flour

kosher salt

FOR THE TOPPING

2 tablespoons unsalted butter

2 sweet onions, peeled and
   thinly sliced

kosher salt

extra-virgin olive oil for
   brushing

2 cups finely grated pecorino

4 whole anchovies (optional)

2 tablespoons salted capers,
   rinsed

5 thin lemon slices

½ teaspoon red pepper flakes

3 sprigs thyme, leaves
   removed from stems and
   stems discarded

3 sprigs Italian flat-leaf
   parsley, leaves removed
   from stems and stems
   discarded

TO MAKE THE DOUGH Fill a liquid measuring cup with the warm water. Add the baker's yeast and let sit for 5 minutes. It should bubble and look gassy. In a large wooden or glass bowl, combine flour and a big pinch of salt. Once the yeast has activated, mix it into the flour with a wooden spoon until the dough pulls away from the bowl. Turn the dough out onto a well-floured surface and knead until the texture is consistent, but no more. Place in an oiled bowl and sprinkle a little flour on top. Drape a clean, moist kitchen towel over the dough and let it rise in a warm place for 1 hour.

TO MAKE THE TOPPING In a large skillet, melt the butter, then add the onions and a pinch of salt. Sauté over medium-low heat for 25 to 30 minutes, or until the onions are caramel colored, stirring occasionally. If they begin to dry up and burn, add a little water to the skillet and turn the heat down to low.

Place a pizza stone on the middle rack of the oven and preheat to 450°F. Once the dough has more than doubled in size, roll it out on a flat, floured surface and stretch it into a round about 9 inches in diameter. Transfer it to a wooden peel or sheet pan. Brush the dough with olive oil and sprinkle the grated pecorino on top. If using, lay the anchovies across the cheese, then evenly distribute the capers, lemon slices, red pepper flakes, and thyme. Slide the tart off the peel onto the stone or slip the sheet pan in the oven. Bake for 20 to 25 minutes, or until the crust is golden brown; turn the tart a few times during baking to evenly brown the edge. Transfer the tart to a cutting board and sprinkle with parsley leaves. Slice into wedges and serve hot.

Mussel Chowder
with Leeks and Heirloom Potatoes

Nothing warms up a cold night like a fresh mussel doused in garlic-scented cream, floating alongside caramelized leeks and soft potatoes. I like to cook shellfish separately from the base of soups and stews for two reasons: one, they can be full of sand when they open, and, two, it's easier to cook them to perfection that way.

SERVES 8 TO 10

2 tablespoons butter

6 leeks, tougher greens removed, whites and light greens thinly sliced

kosher salt

1 garlic head, cloves separated, peeled, and minced

1 tablespoon flour

2 cups white wine

4 cups fish stock

2 pounds heirloom potatoes

2 cups heavy cream

6 sprigs thyme, leaves removed from stems and stems discarded

fresh ground pepper

60 mussels

sea salt

6 sprigs tarragon, leaves removed from stems and roughly chopped

6 sprigs parsley, leaves removed from stems and roughly chopped

In a medium Dutch oven, melt the butter, then stir in the leeks and a pinch of salt. Sauté over medium-low heat, softening the leeks until they break down, about 15 minutes, stirring occasionally. Do not allow them to burn. Add the minced garlic and cook for 5 more minutes. Add flour and, using a wooden spoon, disperse it to evenly coat the leeks and garlic. Pour in wine, turn the heat up to high, and bring to a boil. Reduce to a simmer and cook for 5 minutes, or until the alcohol is cooked off (you will no longer smell it). Add the fish stock and the potatoes and simmer over medium heat until the potatoes are fork-tender, about 15 minutes. Stir in the cream and thyme and simmer for 5 minutes more. Season with salt and pepper to taste. Remove from heat and set aside.

Fill a large lidded pot with an inch of water and bring it to a boil. Add the mussels, cover tightly, and boil over high heat for 3 to 5 minutes. If the water boils over, finish cooking with the cover only partially on. If most of the mussels don't open, shake the pot and boil them partially covered for another minute or two. Once most of the mussels are open, turn the heat off and remove the lid. Do not overcook. Discard any closed or broken mussels.

To plate, fill each bowl with 5 to 6 mussels. Pour the creamy potatoes over the mussels. Season with sea salt and a twist of fresh ground pepper, then garnish with a smattering of tarragon and parsley.

Raw Brussels Sprouts and Kale Salad
with Cranberries and Almonds

Like most root vegetables, a Brussels sprout can be eaten raw only if it is extremely thinly sliced. A mandoline, one of my favorite kitchen tools, can make such thin and even cuts, rendering a fibrous raw root vegetable delicate and digestible. The same goes for kale leaves. This is a hearty and nutritious winter salad, accented with sweet and tart cranberries and crunchy slivered almonds. It makes a delicious lunch all on its own.

SERVES 8

FOR THE SALAD

1 bunch red Russian kale
2 cups Brussels sprouts
¼ cup slivered almonds
¼ cup dried cranberries
1 cup finely grated Parmesan

FOR THE DRESSING

2 garlic cloves, peeled
1 tablespoon grain mustard
2 shallots, peeled and
    minced
zest and juice of 1 lemon
2 tablespoons sherry vinegar
red pepper flakes
5 tablespoons olive oil
kosher salt
fresh ground pepper

TO MAKE THE SALAD Remove the ribs from the kale by holding the leaf stem with one hand and pulling the leaf backward against the rib with the other. Chiffonade the kale leaves. Using a mandoline, shave each Brussels sprout into thin strips, holding the root end and running it through the mandoline while being careful not to cut yourself. To be extra safe, shield your hand by holding the sprout root with a small kitchen towel. Toss the kale and sprouts in a medium salad bowl and keep in the fridge until ready to dress.

TO MAKE THE DRESSING Using a pestle, mash garlic cloves with a pinch of salt in the base of a mortar. Add the grain mustard, minced shallots, lemon zest and juice, sherry vinegar, and red pepper flakes to taste. Stir in the olive oil and season with salt and pepper to taste. Let the flavors mingle for about 20 minutes.

Dress the salad about 10 minutes before you are ready to serve it. Toss together with the almonds, cranberries, and Parmesan cheese.

Duck Breast

with Jacob's Cattle Beans and Roast Apples

Duck is so rich, flavorful, and decadent on its own, it needs only the simplest of accompaniments. In this case, a pot of beans and some roasted apples pair perfectly with the duck breast—a basic preparation fit for the most festive of gatherings. This dish is conducive to a family-style presentation.

SERVES 8

2 cups dry Jacob's Cattle beans, soaked overnight

kosher salt

1 yellow onion, peeled and quartered

2 garlic cloves, peeled

1 bay leaf

2 sweet apples, cored and cut into wedges

4 tablespoons butter, melted

3 large or 4 small duck breasts, room temperature

fresh ground pepper

3 sprigs oregano

In a large pot, cover the beans with plenty of salted water, then add the onion, garlic cloves, and bay leaf. Bring to a simmer over medium-high heat and cook for 45 minutes to 1 hour, or until the beans are tender. Turn off the heat and leave the beans in the water until ready to serve.

Preheat the oven to 400°F. In a medium bowl, toss the apples in the melted butter and a little salt. Line a sheet pan with parchment paper and arrange the apples in a single layer. Roast them for about 15 minutes or until they are golden. Remove the pan from the oven and set aside, but keep the heat at 400°F.

Salt and pepper the duck breasts on both sides and slice shallow perpendicular lines across the fat cap on a bias to allow the fat to render; do not cut all the way through the meat. Lay the breasts fat side down in a large stainless-steel frying pan and cook over medium-low heat for up to 25 minutes. Once the fat is rendered, the breasts will begin to turn golden and crisp up. To finish the breasts, bake them in the 400°F oven in a stainless steel frying pan for 5 to 10 minutes, depending on their size. You will know they are done when they are almost but not quite firm to the touch. Remove them from the oven and let rest on a cooling rack.

When ready to serve, heat up the beans in their liquid. Drain them and arrange them on a large platter. Slice the duck breasts thinly and lay on top of the beans. Spoon the roasted apples around the duck and garnish with green sprigs of oregano.

Chocolate Almond Brandy Cake
with Crème Anglaise

This is my most trusted recipe, one that I have shared with hundreds of people over the years, as it always yields magnificent results. If you use a nut flour, the cake will be light and airy, and if you use coarser ground nuts, the cake texture will have a coarser crumb. Either way, for a flourless chocolate cake, it is light, delicate, and gluten-free.

)

SERVES 8

FOR THE CAKE

butter and cocoa powder
  for preparing the pan
10 ounces semisweet
  chocolate chips
12 tablespoons butter,
  softened to room
  temperature
¾ cup sugar
6 eggs, separated
1¼ cups almond flour or
  finely ground almonds
1 tablespoon brandy
½ teaspoon kosher salt
confectioners' sugar for
  dusting

FOR THE CRÈME ANGLAISE

2 cups heavy cream
1 vanilla bean, pod split
  and seeds scraped out
⅔ cup sugar
6 egg yolks

TO MAKE THE CAKE Preheat the oven to 375°F. Butter the sides of a 9-inch springform pan and dust them with cocoa powder. Then line the bottom with parchment paper. Melt chocolate chips in the top of double boiler over medium heat. With a stand mixer fitted with the whisk attachment, beat the butter and sugar together at medium speed until light and fluffy. Scrape the sides of the bowl once or twice during mixing. Add egg yolks one at a time, beating to fully incorporate. Beat in the melted chocolate while it is still warm. Stir in almond flour or ground almonds and brandy. Transfer the batter to a separate bowl.

Wash the bowl and whisk attachment and rinse in cold water. Place the egg whites and salt in the mixing bowl and beat until stiff peaks form. Carefully fold the whites into the chocolate mixture in thirds until fully incorporated. Pour the batter into the prepared springform pan.

Place the cake pan on a sheet pan to prevent spills. Bake for 15 minutes, then reduce the temperature to 350°F and bake for an additional 30 to 35 minutes. The cake will typically crack down the center about 10 minutes before it is done. It is ready when you insert a toothpick in the cake and it comes out clean.

TO MAKE THE CRÈME ANGLAISE In a medium saucepan, combine the cream, vanilla bean pod, and vanilla seeds and bring just to a simmer over medium heat. Turn off the heat, add the sugar, and stir to dissolve. In a large glass bowl, whisk the egg yolks until they are pale yellow. Slowly add the warm cream mixture into the egg yolks while continuing to whisk. Then pour the egg and cream mixture back into the saucepan. Cook over low heat, stirring continuously, until the custard sauce begins to thicken and coats the back of the spoon, about 6 to 8 minutes. Strain through a fine-mesh sieve. Serve warm or at room temperature.

Place a plate over the top of the springform pan, turn it over, and lift up the mold to release the cake. Peel off parchment paper and carefully move to a cake plate. Dust generously with confectioners' sugar and serve warm or at room temperature, with a small pitcher of crème anglaise.

DECEMBER

THE FULL
COLD MOON

As the days grow shorter and the nights longer, the December full moon signifies the gripping cold that lasts from sundown to sunrise, making the ground impenetrable. Lakes and rivers begin to acquire a thin and growing layer of ice, while animals take refuge in their dens to hibernate. With every new snowfall come plenty of outdoor activities, everything from snowshoeing to cross-country skiing to ice-skating. Spending the days bundled up and playing outdoors builds a hearty appetite by the time the sun sets.

Back at the house, it's time to get the fire going something fierce. As December is still an excellent month for oysters, I'll often pick up a few dozen at the fish shop and offer them to my guests as an appetizer. They need little more than a swig of champagne or a cold beer as accompaniment. There is camaraderie in putting everyone to work, which—let's be honest—is no work at all. As the meal effortlessly begins to come together, we laugh heartily about who was the least coordinated on a pair of skis or took the hardest fall. The dogs lie at our feet, exhausted, dreaming of sniffing through the woods or of running across the frozen ponds. These are brilliant days, when our only obligation is to relax and bask in the warmth and merriment of good friends, with food and drink in hand.

What luck that the festive holidays coincide with this dark and frigid month of December. (Or perhaps it's been by design all along.) The December Full Moon Supper menu brings us in from the cold, in more ways than one. This meal can be enjoyed in jeans and sweaters on a snowy afternoon or for a dressed-up evening affair. No matter what your attire, remember to give thanks to the final full moon of the year and prepare for the annual cycle to renew itself yet again.

DECEMBER
·
FULL MOON SUPPER
MENU

Champagne
217

Oysters Rockefeller
219

Chestnut Soup
with a Spoonful of Cream
220

Bitter Greens, Parsley Leaf,
Celery, and Pumpkin Seeds
with Pomegranate Vinaigrette
223

Cast-Iron Rib Eyes
with Rosemary Butter and Celery
Root and Parsnip Gratin
224

Linzer Torte
of Ground Hazelnuts and
Raspberry Jam
228

Champagne

One of the best features of the holiday season is its call for celebration in liquid form—in other words, champagne. Serve whatever you can afford, but shoot for something dry rather than sweet. And if true French champagne is out of your budget, try an exceptional cava, prosecco, or my favorite, sparkling Vouvray.

FESTIVELY SERVES 8

1 bottle good champagne

Chill 8 tall stemmed wineglasses or champagne flutes. Fill each a third of the way with bubbly, wait 30 seconds, and then pour another third on top. The first pour will act as a pillow to the second, diffusing some of the bubbles. No need to fill the glass to the top, as you need a little extra room for the liquid to slosh around when it comes time to toast.

Oysters Rockefeller

This is a perfect dish for the holidays. The savory bread crumbs absorb the salty brine of the oyster and the flavors penetrate the body of the oyster.

$$\smile$$

SERVES 8 TO 10

8 strips thick bacon, each cut into ¼-inch pieces

4 tablespoons butter

2 shallots, peeled and minced

kosher salt

½ loaf day-old country bread, finely chopped in a food processor

pinch fresh ground pepper

1 handful savory herbs, finely chopped (rosemary, thyme, savory, and parsley)

12 oysters, shucked (reserve shells and as much of the liquor as possible)

Preheat the oven to 400°F. In a large cast-iron frying pan, render bacon over medium-low heat. Once the meat begins to crisp, remove with a slotted spoon and set aside. With the heat still on medium low, melt the butter in the pan, add the shallots and a pinch of salt, and sauté for 5 minutes, until the shallots are soft. Mix in the bread crumbs, pepper, and savory herbs. Reintroduce the bacon to the pan. Cook over medium heat for 5 minutes, or until bread crumbs are golden.

Arrange the shucked oysters in an ovenproof serving vessel with a rim, such as a rimmed platter. Spoon about a tablespoon of stuffing in each oyster shell and set them around the oyster bodies, nestled into the oyster liquor. Bake until the liquid is bubbling and the bread crumbs are toasty and golden brown, about 5 to 7 minutes. Serve immediately.

HOW TO SHUCK AN OYSTER

1. Place the oyster inside an old dish towel, exposing the pointed tip to the east. Hold the towel firmly over the oyster and angle the tip downward.
2. Place the oyster knife into the tip of the oyster and slowly work it back and forth in between the shells. Once you have some purchase, use leverage to open and release the shells.
3. Slide the knife into the oyster and then turn the tip up so that you can see the knife coming out of the shell. Twist to release the other two fastening points on the oyster. Continue twisting the knife to reveal the body of the oyster. Move the knife to the back end of the oyster, shaving the body off the muscle that fastens it to the top shell. Remove the top shell.
4. Run the knife under the body of the oyster, releasing it from the muscle on the bottom shell. Use your (clean) finger to get rid of any shell or sediment.

Chestnut Soup
with a Spoonful of Cream

Chestnuts don't make their way into the markets in Maine until the holidays. I always look forward to scooping a few pounds of them from the basket and roasting them fireside. Be forewarned, however, that peeling chestnuts is not the easiest of tasks. If you're cooking the rest of the meal, it's a good idea to delegate peeling to family members or friends who are willing to help as they're waiting to be fed.

SERVES 8

two 14-ounce jars whole roasted and shelled chestnuts or 3 pounds chestnuts in their shells

2 tablespoons olive oil

2 medium yellow onions, peeled and cut into medium-size dice

3 carrots, cut in half lengthwise and then across every ¼ inch

3 celery ribs, cut into ¼-inch pieces

kosher salt

1 garlic clove, peeled and minced

½ cup sherry

12 cups chicken stock

1 bay leaf

fresh ground pepper

½ cup locally sourced unpasteurized cream, room temperature

If you are using whole chestnuts, with a paring knife cut an X on the flat side of each chestnut, piercing the shell. Then place the chestnuts in a cast-iron pan and roast over medium heat on the stovetop or on an open fire, until they begin to soften in the middle, about 15 to 20 minutes. You will have to open one and cut into it to tell if they are soft. You will need to turn them frequently to promote even roasting. Let them cool slightly, then remove them from their shells piece by piece (it helps to have many hands) and set aside.

In a medium heavy-bottomed soup pot, warm the olive oil and add the onions, carrots, celery, and a pinch of salt. Cover and sweat the vegetables over medium-low heat until the onions are translucent, about 10 to 15 minutes. Add the garlic, cover, and sweat for another 5 minutes. Uncover and add the sherry. (If cooking on a gas stove, turn the flame off first to prevent the alcohol from igniting.) Turn the heat up to medium high and cook until the alcohol has evaporated, about 5 minutes. Add the chestnuts (if using preserved chestnuts, drain and rinse them first), along with the chicken stock and bay leaf. Bring to a boil, reduce to a simmer, and cook until the chestnuts are tender, about 15 minutes.

In a blender puree the soup in batches, seasoning with salt and pepper as you go. Bring the pureed soup batches together in one vessel and reheat, tasting for seasoning one more time.

To serve, ladle into individual bowls and drizzle a spoonful of cream atop each bowl.

Bitter Greens, Parsley Leaf, Celery, and Pumpkin Seeds

with Pomegranate Vinaigrette

While the greens aisle at the grocery store can be a sad scene in winter, you can usually find a crisp bunch of bitter greens, such as endive and red radicchio, which can serve as the base of bold winter salad. A little parsley adds robust flavor, and celery, sliced elegantly on a bias, lends texture. Seeds from a rather festive winter fruit, the pomegranate, offer a pop of color—and all of a sudden, you've transformed a drab winter's day into a magnificent display of winter's offerings.

SERVES 8

1 garlic clove, peeled

kosher salt

2 tablespoons pomegranate juice (see "How to Open a Pomegranate" on p. 37)

2 tablespoons red wine vinegar

1 tablespoon Dijon mustard

juice and zest of 1 small lemon

⅓ cup olive oil

3 endives, cut across into ¼-inch rounds

1 head radicchio, leaves removed from the head and ripped into large bite-size pieces

1 bunch parsley, leaves picked from stems and stems discarded

8 celery ribs, cut on a diagonal into 1-inch pieces

seeds of ½ pomegranate

2 tablespoons pumpkin seeds

With a mortar and pestle, grind the garlic clove with a pinch of salt until it resembles a paste. Stir in the pomegranate juice, red wine vinegar, Dijon mustard, and lemon zest and juice. Gradually beat in the olive oil with the pestle. Let the dressing sit for 30 minutes, until the flavors meld.

In a large salad bowl, combine the endive, radicchio, parsley, and celery. Add a few spoonfuls of the dressing and give the salad a toss. Sprinkle the pomegranate seeds and pumpkin seeds on top, adding some brilliant color to an already beautiful mix of greens. Serve with remaining dressing on the side.

Cast-Iron Rib Eyes
with Rosemary Butter and Celery Root and Parsnip Gratin

While I cannot in good conscience recommend eating large quantities of meat—let alone choice cuts—on a regular basis, a big, fat, juicy rib eye is perfect for rare and special occasions. This recipe suggests one rib eye for every two or three people. Here, the meat is cooked simply in cast iron with olive oil, salt, and pepper. If you are eating a quality piece of meat, that's all you need.

SERVES 8

3 tablespoons olive oil

4 bone-in rib eyes

kosher salt

fresh ground pepper

8 tablespoons (1 stick) butter, softened

½ lemon

3 sprigs rosemary, leaves separated from stems and roughly chopped, stems discarded, plus 3 more sprigs for garnish

sea salt

Preheat the oven to 425°F. Line a sheet pan with aluminum foil. In a large cast-iron pan, heat 2 tablespoons of the olive oil. Season the rib eyes with salt and pepper. Over medium-high heat, sear two of the steaks on each side until golden brown, 6 to 8 minutes. The meat will release itself from the pan once a proper crust has formed. Then flip and cook for another 4 to 5 minutes. Transfer the cooked steaks to the sheet pan. Sear the remaining two steaks with the rest of the olive oil, then transfer to the sheet pan. Bake the steaks until rare or a meat thermometer registers 130°F, 4 to 5 minutes, depending on the thickness of the steaks. Remove from the oven and let them rest for at least 5 minutes. Residual heat will cook it to medium rare.

In a small bowl, fold the chopped rosemary into the softened butter and chill in the refrigerator until ready to serve.

When it is time to serve the steaks, carve them into strips against the grain and arrange them on a platter. Squeeze lemon juice over the top and spoon a little rosemary butter on the meat, allowing the residual heat to melt the butter. Season with a few sprinkles of sea salt and garnish the platter with the additional rosemary sprigs. Serve with Celery Root and Parsnip Gratin (see recipe on page 227).

CELERY ROOT AND PARSNIP GRATIN

The making of good gratin takes time, and the result produces a heavy dose
of calories. Some cooks boil the root vegetables ahead of time, shortening the
cook time and minimizing the amount of milk and cream necessary to cook
the vegetables through. I prefer the traditional method, used here. A gratin can
be made in a number of vessels: a glass baking dish, a copper pan, or a ceramic
baking dish. Most important, the vegetables must fit properly in the vessel.
For this recipe, I use an 8-by-8-inch glass or ceramic baking dish.

SERVES 8

4 tablespoons butter

4 garlic cloves, peeled and
minced

2 cups milk

2 cups cream

2 celery roots, thinly sliced
on a mandoline

4 parsnips, thinly sliced on
a mandoline

2 cups grated Parmesan

8 sprigs thyme, leaves
picked from stems and
stems discarded

kosher salt

fresh ground pepper

Preheat the oven to 350°F. Melt the butter in a small
saucepan over low heat and cook the garlic in it until it
softens. Watch it carefully; you don't want it to gain any
color at all. Whisk the garlic and butter into a 4-cup
liquid measuring cup along with the milk and cream.
Add a ladleful of the garlic cream to the base of an
8-by-8-inch baking dish. Layer the celery root across
the bottom of the dish, overlapping each piece by about
½ inch. Scatter the parsnips in another layer, covering
the celery root. Sprinkle the root vegetables with a
third of the Parmesan and thyme and season with salt
and pepper. Pour another ladle or two of garlic cream
evenly over the cheese. Repeat this process 2 or 3 times
before reaching the top of the dish. Don't hesitate to
press the ingredients down into the baking dish if necessary to make more room. The cream should fill the
baking dish about three-quarters of the way to the top.
Finish with a sprinkling of cheese.

Cover the gratin with aluminum foil. This will allow
the vegetables to steam and cook through faster. Bake
for 1 hour. Remove the foil and bake for another 25 to
30 minutes, until the gratin browns on top. Remove
from the oven and let it cool for at least 10 minutes.
Cut into squares and serve hot.

Linzer Torte
of Ground Hazelnuts and Raspberry Jam

I've never been much of a Christmas cookie fan: they're covered with all that sugar and sticky icing, are not terribly flavorful, and are extremely time-consuming to prepare. But a Linzer torte always gets my attention around the holidays, especially since I can use it as an excuse to open a jar of homemade raspberry jam, preserved from the summer.

SERVES 8 TO 9

1 cup hazelnuts
¾ cup all-purpose flour
½ cup whole wheat flour
12 tablespoons butter, softened
¼ cup brown sugar
½ cup white sugar
1 egg
½ teaspoon vanilla extract
½ teaspoon kosher salt
one 10-ounce jar raspberry jam

Preheat the oven to 350°F. Lay the hazelnuts across a sheet pan and toast in the oven for 8 minutes, or until they begin to smell nutty. Transfer to a food processor and pulse them to a fine texture.

In a medium mixing bowl, combine the ground hazelnuts, all-purpose flour, and whole wheat flour. In the bowl of a stand mixer with a whisk attachment, beat the butter with the brown sugar and white sugar. Add the egg and the vanilla extract and beat to incorporate, scraping down the sides of the bowl with a spatula. Add the dry ingredients to the bowl and whisk everything together on medium speed to make a dough.

Line the bottom of an 8-by-8-inch baking dish with parchment paper. Press two-thirds of the dough into the base of the dish, making a ridge around the outside tall enough to contain the jam. Empty the jar of raspberry jam onto the dough and spread across evenly. On a flat, floured surface, roll the remaining dough into a long, flat rectangle, about 8 by 4 inches. Cut lengthwise into four strips and lay them across the torte, two in one direction and two in the other, like a tic-tac-toe board. Refrigerate the torte for 20 minutes, then bake for 45 minutes, or until the crust is golden brown and the jam is bubbling. To prevent the jam from spilling over the sides, let the torte cool fully before serving.

ACKNOWLEDGMENTS

First and foremost, I'd like to thank my editor, Rochelle Bourgault, who persuaded me to write the Full Moon Suppers cookbook, which turned out to be the perfect foray into cookbook publishing. I'd also like to thank the people at Roost Books for taking a chance on a first-time author and encouraging me to "make it mine." This book would not have the look and feel that it does were it not for Daniel Urban-Brown, the art director, and his team of designers at Roost.

Five years ago, while writing restaurant reviews for *Maine Magazine*, I met Kristin Teig, a food and lifestyle photographer whose work was quickly gaining a national following. We agreed to one day craft a cookbook together, and this book is our resulting baby. I've never had so much fun working with someone, and I hope that this is the first of many books we produce together. I'd also like to thank Sonia Turek, a student of mine at Salt Water Farm Cooking School, who happens to also have been an editor for the *Boston Globe* for much of her career. She provided a second set of eyes on every word of this book before it was submitted, and with my (occasional) lack of attention to detail, it was a very necessary edit. She also graciously tested many of the recipes for friends and family, providing excellent feedback.

Credit must be given to my dear friends Alex-Rhuland Syquia and Eric Thornton, who developed the bar program at my restaurant, providing the inspiration for many of the cocktails in this book. And then there are all of those who helped me produce the Full Moon Suppers, a list that is far too long for this page, but you know who you are. Thanks for making magic with me beneath the light of the full moon.

INDEX

ABOUT THE AUTHOR

Annemarie Ahearn founded Salt Water Farm in 2009, a cooking school for home cooks on Maine's Penobscot Bay. She began her studies at Colorado College, when her interest in food developed while living in Aix-en-Provence, where she studied Provincial cuisine and visited the open-air markets. She later apprenticed in the kitchen at Le Jardin Notre Dame in Paris. While living in New York Ahearn worked in the editorial department of *Saveur* magazine and wrote the bi-weekly food column "Downtown Chef" for *The L Magazine*. After graduating from the Institute of Culinary Education with a degree in both culinary arts and culinary management, she worked for Dan Barber at Blue Hill Restaurant, as personal assistant to Tom Colicchio of Craft Restaurants, and as a personal chef in New York. She also worked at the Slow Food Headquarters. Before opening Salt Water Farm, she taught classes at Cook and Taste, a small, recreational cooking school in Barcelona. Ahearn was named one of the "40 Big Food Thinkers 40 and Under" in *Food & Wine* magazine, "changing the way America eats."

In 2013 Ahearn opened Salt Water Farm Cafe & Market in Rockport Harbor, Maine, offering locally sourced fare for breakfast, lunch, and dinner, and has garnered acclaim in the *Wall Street Journal*, the *New York Times*, and the *Boston Globe*, as well as in *Bon Appétit*, *DownEast Magazine*, and *Maine Magazine*. She is also a contributing writer for *DownEast Magazine*, sharing recipes from her school, and regularly teaches cooking skills to high school students in her community through the Back to Basics program.

ROOST BOOKS
An imprint of Shambhala Publications, Inc.
4720 Walnut Street
Boulder, Colorado 80301
roostbooks.com

9 8 7 6 5 4 3 2 1

First Edition
Printed in China

♾This edition is printed on acid-free paper that meets
the American National Standards Institute Z39.48
Standard.
♻ Shambhala Publications makes every effort to print
on recycled paper. For more information please visit
www.shambhala.com.

Distributed in the United States by
Penguin Random House LLC and in Canada by
Random House of Canada Ltd

Designed by Liz Quan

Library of Congress Cataloging-in-Publication Data

Names: Ahearn, Annemarie, author. | Teig, Kristin,
photographer. | Salt Water Farm (Rockport Harbor, Me.)
Title: Full moon suppers at Salt Water Farm: recipes from
land and sea / Annemarie Ahearn; photographs
by Kristin Teig.
Other titles: Fullmoon suppers at Salt Water Farm
Description: First edition. | Boulder: Roost Books, [2017] |
Includes index.
Identifiers: LCCN 2016015864 | ISBN 9781611803327
(hardcover: alk. paper)
Subjects: LCSH: Seasonal cooking. | Cooking, American—
New England style. | Cooking (Seafood) | Salt Water
Farm (Rockport Harbor, Me.) | LCGFT: Cookbooks.
Classification: LCC TX714 .A432155 2017 | DDC
641.5/64—dc23 LC record available at https://lccn.loc
.gov/2016015864